COCKTAILS

The subtle art of mixing well

Published 1983 by Hamlyn Publishing Group Limited
London · New York · Sydney · Toronto
Astronaut House, Feltham, Middlesex, England.

Designed for Lansdowne International by
VanBeek Design Limited, Maidenhead, Berks.

ISBN 0 600 32382 X

Printed in Spain by Printer industria gráfica sa
Sant Vicenç dels Horts Barcelona D.L.B. 29079-1983

COCKTAILS

The subtle art of mixing well

Introduced and edited by Desmond Marwood with
additional picture comment by Paul Drennan
Photography by Julian Bajzert

HAMLYN
London · New York · Sydney · Toronto

CONTENTS

Introduction	10
What is a cocktail?	11
Setting up a bar	12
Bar equipment	13
Bottled stock	14
Glassware	15
Measures	16
General hints & tips	17
Gin based recipes	19
Whisky based recipes	37
Vodka based recipes	53
Brandy based recipes	67
Rum based recipes	83
Champagne based — Aperitif recipes	95
Other classic types	107
Tequila recipes	114
Non-alcoholic recipes	115
Glossary	120
Index	122

BLUE BLAZER

He had never punted in his life before.
Slowly and carefully, she showed him how it was done. He was a quick learner.
After a while she giggled and said he navigated as well as anyone she knew.
He blushed and shivered and shook another Blue Blazer cocktail.
She toasted the evening sun, and after a while they moved off again. Going downstream.
"There's a lot to be said in favour of flat-bottomed boats," he said wistfully.
"Yes," she smiled. "But you wait until we reach the rapids."

Of all the bars, in all the world, the bars labelled 'Cocktail' are those we have come to associate with a particular form of luxurious relaxation reserved for making idle gossip, whilst sipping seemingly exotic drinks as though time and money never mattered, and maybe surviving from one or two new alcoholic experiences along the way. Soft lights, muffled decor, the gentle tinkle of a keyboard, and the sensually rythmic swish of ice, all contribute to the awakening of taste buds, and the stimulation of heightened expectancy.

Like the Great Mixologist that he is, the friendly bartender stands against the chrome and glassware of an illuminated backdrop, to shake another liquid masterpiece for mankind's delectation. How we envy the man his job satisfaction, his knowledgeable skills, and the self-fulfilment he derives from his creative task. Never forget that the mixing of cocktails is a delicate matter, regarded by many as practically an art form. However good an original recipe might be, bad mixing or poor presentation can be the ruin of any cocktail.

Presentation is part of a good cocktail.

Mixing and presentation then, are just two important factors to keep in mind if you wish to simulate a Cocktail Bar setting in your own home for the intimate enjoyment of family and friends. The purpose of this book is to help you in achieving this pleasurable objective. With plenty of practice, there's really nothing to stop anyone becoming a proficient mixer, and thereby discovering themselves to be an excitingly new type of host or hostess. It will take time to learn the recipes and perfect the techniques, but never despair.

It's unlikely that anyone has ever learned, or would even be able to collect, a truly comprehensive list of cocktail recipes. Their number is virtually limitless, and professional and amateur mixers throughout the world are continually creating new drinks.

Who knows — maybe you'll be experimenting and inventing your own new cocktail recipes in no time at all. Creating a new cocktail to commemorate a birthday, anniversary, or some other intimate happening, can add spice to any celebration.

A modern cocktail can be defined as a drink composed of at least two ingredients which have been shaken or stirred together, and served as either a long or a short drink.

Doubtless, mankind has been enjoying mixed drinks composed of such things as spiced wines, and other ingredients, throughout the ages. It is now generally accepted, however, that the modern cocktail is yet another of the U.S. of A's gifts unto the world. The first authentic reference to cocktail in print, appeared in the New York periodical *Balance*, issue dated 13 May, 1806, when it was recorded that. . . "Cocktail is a kind of stimulating liquor, composed of spirits of any kind, sugar, water, and bitters — it is vulgarly called bittered sling, and is supposed to be an excellent electioneering potion". American folklore traces the coining of the word "cocktail" in reference to drink back to the year 1776, when the bar of a Yorktown tavern was reported to have been decorated (for some unknown reason) with large bunches of birds' tailfeathers hanging up around the place.

A complete list of cocktail recipes would be limitless.

A drunken regular raised his head and blearily called for "a glass of those cocktails"!

Good humouredly, barmaid Betsy Flanagan served him with a mixed drink of random content, the only positively known ingredient having been a tailfeather which she plucked from a decorative bunch, and popped into the concoction. It was much later, during the dry period of the prohibition, that liquor starved Americans of more recent times, were forced to apply their ingenuity to the improvement of whatever quality of limited alcohol there was available. To make it more palatable, they mixed it with other ingredients and gave birth to many new cocktail mixtures which evolved as specialities associated with that fast-living era.

It's fun to remember that your bar should be one part of the home which really reflects your own personality, imagination, or maybe sense of humour.

There are three main categories of home Cocktail Bar — the Mobile, the Semi-Permanent, and the Permanent.

The Mobile Bar is usually stored away somewhere, and wheeled out as required to any part of the house, inside or out, in which you might be entertaining guests. Apart from limited shelf and storage space, the main disadvantages of the Mobile Bar, is its lack of fresh water washing facilities for glassware.

The Semi-Permanent Bar is usually an item of displayed furniture placed in whichever room has been chosen as the home's main reception area. Wherever that may be, it's advisable to pick a location as near as is convenient to washing facilities. Otherwise such bars, or cocktail cabinets as they are sometimes called, often provide good storage space and display areas, and some are even illuminated.

The Permanent Bar is what the name implies — a permanent structure, and an integral part of any room into which it is built. Whilst its design and erection presents the biggest challenge, it also provides the greatest opportunity to build something which is both functional and attractive. All of it is well within the capabilities of the average do-it-yourself home handyman.

Before cluttering up a bar with non-essential luxuries, make sure your Permanent Bar is plumbed for a sink with hot and cold running water, and a refrigerator should be installed. Illumination of the bar is an effective component, and whilst a lighting scheme should be subdued, it needs to be arranged so that it shows off bottles and equipment in the most attractive and eye-catching manner.

It could be that the main lighting of the rest of the room in which the Permanent Bar is erected, will need to be adjusted on occasions when the bar is in use, if the full and cosy intimacy of a cocktail lounge is to be effectively simulated.

Whichever type of bar you decide to develop, some basics are common to the design and building of each and every type. For example, bottles and glassware are always most effectively displayed on shelves of clear, or colour-tinted glass, according to your fancy. Any type of bar can be designed and built using easily available materials such as fresh timber, plasticised panelling, natural logs, old beer barrels, packing cases, bricks, stones, restored or converted pieces of old furniture (such as wardrobes or pianos), or anything which appeals to your imagination, or perhaps could be associated with a theme.

To design and build a Mobile Bar to a theme may be a bit restrictive, but the design of a Semi-Permanent, or better still Permanent Bar, can reflect the owner's interest in matters seafaring, fishing, golf, motoring, music, western films, honky-tonk, or any hobby or madcap interest.

And of course, any Permanent Bar aspirants will have the additional challenge of devising thematic ideas for ingeniously inspired bar stools. Then, there's also scope for preparing a tape of suitable background music. . .

Regardless of the type or theme of any Cocktail Bar, it should be equipped with the following basic items. . .

Bar Shaker; popular types named the 'Standard', 'Boston', or 'America'; alternatively, use an electric blender — if you don't mind losing the allurement of that ol' manual-shaking magic.

Cloths; one for drying glasses, the other for wiping down work surfaces.

Fruit Knife and Chopping Board; for citrus fruit slicing, also substituting as reserve cheese board.

Ice Bucket (with tongs); preferably insulated, and sufficiently large to contain a substantial amount of ice cubes.

Mixing Glass; be on safe side, and stock both a medium and a large glass, or jug (with long-handled spoon for stirring).

Spirit Measures (see Measures, Page 16).

Strainer; for use when pouring from mix container.

Additionally, the proficient bartender requires to have handy. . .

Bottle Opener	Limes
Can Opener	Maraschino Cherries
Castor Sugar	Nutmeg
Cinnamon	Olives
Cocktail Onions	Oranges
Corkscrew	Salted Peanuts
Eggs	Salt and Pepper
Fruit Squeezer	Serviettes
Lemons	Soda Syphon
Straws	Swizzle Sticks
Toothpicks	

Bar Equipment can become very expensive . . .

Try running a Cocktail Bar on a skimpy list of bottled stock and you'll negate any hope of acquiring that Mister Master Mixer reputation.

On the other hand, whilst there's no need for madness, investment in bottled stock might include the following spirits, liqueurs and carbonates . . .

Advokaat	Ginger Ale
Apricot Brandy	Grand Marnier
Cherry Brandy	Grenadine
Angostura Bitters	Gin
Benedictine	Kahlva
Bourbon Whiskey	Maraschino
Brandy	Orange Bitters
Cognac	Orgeat Syrup
Chartreuse	Pernod
Champagne	Soda Water
Cointreau	Sweet Vermouth
Crème de Cassis	Triple Sec
Crème de Menthe	Tomato Juice
Crème de Cacao	Tonic Water
Dark Rum	Tequila
Dry Vermouth	Vodka
Drambuie	White Rum
Eau-de-vie	Whisky (Scotch)
Galliano	Whiskey (Rye)

Some of the bottled stock that might be required.

Don't be too alarmed at the extent of this list. Few would go out and invest in such bottled stock right across the board. Far more judicious to begin by purchasing only the beverages you'll require to mix whatever area of cocktails with which you have decided to begin your experimenting.

Then, gradually (and enjoyably), you can extend your stock in keeping with whatever is to be the expected output of your bar.

Assuming that your Cocktail Bar is to dispense nothing but cocktails, then maybe you'd get away with stocking up with nothing but three or four-ounce, straight-sided, V-shaped cocktail glasses.

However, a Cocktail Bar must be prepared to serve also any tippler who might favour a simple beer, or glass of white wine. So, a well-equipped bar should stock suitably shaped glassware in which to serve both red and white wine, whisky, brandy, beer, liqueur, Old Fashioned, highballs, champagne, and sherry, in addition to V-shaped cocktail glasses.

As with your bottled stock listing on Page 14, don't be alarmed or daunted by this lengthy and expensive list. Again, begin by purchasing only that which you require to start you off, and friends and relatives should thereafter never be stuck what to buy for you as a birthday or Christmas gift.

Another big consideration which will control and limit your need to acquire any particular range of bottled stock or glassware, is the type of bar you are kitting out. Obviously, the Mobile Bar must be fairly specialised, and maybe even restricted. Maybe there's room to be a little more ambitious with a Semi-Permanent Bar, and of course the sky's the limit with the Permanent Bar.

Glassware from left to right: champagne, brandy balloon, cocktail, old-fashioned, martini, liqueur, goblet, highball, wine.

Presentation apart, it could be that your early mixes may not be so good, and they'll need all the help they can get from any source if they're going to have any desirable affect upon the consumer.

The use of fine glassware will also encourage you to care for it in the proper manner. You must learn the ritual of washing each piece separately in hot water, and drying the glass with a cloth whilst it's still remaining warm from the water. Glasses should be highly polished with a cloth, being held by the stem (or even the base), to avoid the appearance of unsightly fingerprints. Then, they should be left to air off completely before being placed back onto their storage shelves. Aside from quality, and the care with which you handle glassware, there's the style which you purchase in the first place. Here, you must conform with custom if you ever hope to be taken seriously as a server of drinks, and ensure that certain drinks are served only in glasses of particular shapes.

Many amateur and professional mixers may be right in advocating the free pouring of ingredients to be the best way of measuring quantities. After all, we've already recognised that the business of mixing a cocktail is an art form. Perhaps it might be served best by the uninhibited flair of the individual who is just a fraction more heavy-handed with one ingredient than another.

It takes much practice, though, to pour freely and repetitively with any accuracy. Also, any cocktail can just as easily be ruined by over or under-measuring any ingredient, for a vital secret of good mixing is to retain a balance and ensure that one ingredient does not drown another. It's advisable then, at least to set out by paying some respect to the need for accuracy of measurement, and to make use of one or any of the several types of spirit measuring devices which are available in many departmental stores.

You'll come across recipes in which ingredients are quantified in imperial fluid ounces, maybe metric millilitres (or both), or maybe just vague references to 'measures'. All of these are perfectly all right, providing you have possession of the appropriate measuring tool. If not, then the need for a mathematical conversion exercise coming between a thirsty person and a quenching drink, can be a very disturbing experience.

So, in order that readers can easily interpret the recipes presented within this book, the quantities of liquid ingredients are specified in 'measures' (or, alternatively as multiples, or parts of a measure). The measure we have adopted as a standard, is the one-sixth of a gill measure of the type available in shops, or which can be ordered directly from the suppliers. A larger measure containing one-third of a gill, twice the amount, can also be obtained.

Reference in our recipes to '1 msr.', then, refers to that contained in the one-sixth of a gill measure, and '2 msrs.' refers to two of those measures, or a single one-third of a gill measure.

Bartenders who are used to this standard of measure, advise that one-sixth of a gill is only marginally less than a single fluid ounce, or 25-30 millilitres. These comparisons will enable our recipes to be transposed easily into metric.

Recipes of any sort which refer to "a dash" of anything, mean just that. It amounts to no more than a flick of the wrist of the hand holding the bottle.

All these measuring principles should suffice adequately until the nonchalant manner displayed by the free pourer has been mastered. Practice is essential if you aspire to such heights, and one way is to begin by topping up any used 750 millilitre bottle with water. Pour one accurate amount from a measure into the first glass, and then try to repeat accurately by pouring a similar amount into each of the remaining thirty or so glasses you will have arrayed and have ready for the exercise. This way, you'll get the knack of pouring accurately the thirty one-sixth of a gill measures, or the twenty-five 30 millilitre measures it will take to empty the bottle.

It's not regarded as a mortal sin to serve up cocktails which might be a bit on the heavy side (providing you don't send your guests off home in a completely smashed state), but at the same time you don't want to be accused of penny-pinching on the hard stuff.

Before your first party begins, remind yourself of two golden rules which must be adhered to when mixing cocktails. . .
STIR with ice, all clear drinks *not* containing fruit juice, cream, or milk.

SHAKE by hand (or powered blender) all drinks containing fruit juice, cream, or milk, in order to acquire a perfect blend.

Here are some further tips which will help your efforts to be recognised, or even admired. . .

○Always pour cocktails into chilled glasses.

○If ice is used to chill glasses, always remove before pouring in drink.

○Keep plenty of fresh ice available at the bar.

○Wrap ice cubes in a towel and smash with mallet (dangerous to use a bottle) to obtain crushed ice.

○Keep orange, lemon and lime slices fresh by covering with a damp cloth and storing in the refrigerator.

○Use fresh fruit juices whenever possible.

○When cutting orange, or lemon peel, shave off only the coloured skin surface in strips of about half to three-quarters of an inch wide.

○Cherries, or any peel, are always added to the cocktail after mixing.

○When filling the shaker, leave room for shaking, use a short, sharp action, and do not rock the mixer.

○Serve cocktails immediately before they are to be consumed.

○If any recipe demands a twist of lemon, or orange peel, first squeeze the peel onto the top of the cocktail, and then drop the peel into the drink.

○Any carbonates should be the last ingredient added to any drink.

○Always consider teetotal guests and car drivers, and have some non-alcoholic drinks available.

○To extract the maximum juice from any fruit, give it a good soak in hot water before squeezing.

○It's worth saving the bartender time trying to dissolve sugar in any drinks requiring this ingredient, by pre-mixing a bottle of sugar syrup and keeping it in the refrigerator. Simply mix one cup of sugar with one cup of water, bring to the boil, simmer until the sugar has dissolved, and allow to cool.

Colourful garnishes can be appetising.

During the 17th century a Dutch doctor combined alcohol with the juniper berry to produce what was considered to be a new medicine for the treatment of patients suffering from certain kidney complaints. Whilst there appears to be little or no record of what happened to the doctor's patients, it is known that subsequent generations of quite healthy folk have been quick to acquire a taste for the medicine gin, which acquired its name from the French word 'genievre', meaning juniper. Some of England's finest Tudor troops even admitted, on returning home from the wars, that this 'gin' had given them what was called 'dutch' courage in the face of the enemy. This is may be one reason some still refer to the spirit by the name Holland.

Over countless years that followed, gin acquired an undesirable reputation as the opium of the poor masses. It became known also as Mother's Ruin because of the belief that the juniper berry content of the drink would bring about an abortion if gin was taken in sufficient quantity, and thereby control the number of mouths to be fed.

However, as late as the lifting of prohibition in America, there came about the popularity of the Dry Martini and with it some respectability for the consumption of gin.

The distillation of gin in modern times has become a more scientific process than the preparation of what was originally quite a simple compound. Now, there are several kinds of gin, with various distillers each claiming that only well kept secrets preserve the individuality of their particular product.

London Dry Gin is probably the most commonly used gin. Old Tom (scarcely produced any more) is very sweet, and Plymouth Gin (produced by only a single distiller) is unsweetened and the only correct variety for use when mixing a Pink Gin. Dutch Gin, whether young or old, has too much of a distinctive flavour to be used in any mixed drink.

CUPID'S BOW

¼ msr. GIN	¼ msr. PASSION FRUIT JUICE
¼ msr. FORBIDDEN FRUIT	CRACKED ICE
¼ msr. AURUM	

Shake ice with all ingredients, and strain off to serve.

ABBEY COCKTAIL

2 msrs. GIN	1 dash ITALIAN VERMOUTH
1 msr. ORANGE JUICE	CRACKED ICE
1 dash ANGOSTURA BITTERS	1 MARASCHINO CHERRY

Shake ice with gin, bitters, orange juice and vermouth. Strain off into cocktail glass and add cherry before serving.

Left to right: Cupid's Bow, Abbey, Alaska, Blériot.

ALASKA COCKTAIL

2 msrs. GIN	ICE
¾ msr. YELLOW CHARTREUSE	LEMON PEEL

Stir ice with gin and Chartreuse, and strain into cocktail glass. Add twist of lemon peel before serving.

BLÉRIOT COCKTAIL

½ msr. GIN	⅛ msr. PEACH BITTERS
¼ msr. DRY VERMOUTH	1 MARASCHINO CHERRY
⅛ msr. CHERRY BRANDY	CRACKED ICE

Stir gin, dry vermouth, Cherry Brandy and peach bitters in ice in mixing glass until mixture becomes cold. Strain off into cocktail glass and decorate with cherry before serving.

GILROY COCKTAIL

½ msr. GIN	¼ msr. LEMON JUICE
½ msr. CHERRY BRANDY	1 dash ORANGE BITTERS
¼ msr. FRENCH VERMOUTH	CRACKED ICE

Shake ice with gin, lemon juice, Cherry Brandy, vermouth and bitters. Strain off into cocktail glass and serve.

GIBSON SWEET

¾ msr. GIN	¾ msr. ITALIAN VERMOUTH
CRACKED ICE	PICKLED ONION

Stir ice with gin and vermouth, and strain into chilled cocktail glass exactly as for Gibson Dry. See page 32.

FRENCH 75

1½ msrs. DRY GIN	1 teaspoon POWDERED SUGAR
3 msrs. CHAMPAGNE	CRACKED ICE
juice of ½ LEMON	LEMON TWIST

Shake ice with combined gin, sugar and lemon juice. Strain onto ice in highball glass. Top up with champagne (taking care not to stir, and thereby retaining effervescence), and add a twist of lemon before serving.

Left to right: Gilroy, Gibson Sweet, French 75, Fallen Angel.

FALLEN ANGEL COCKTAIL

1½ msrs. GIN	juice of ½ LEMON
2 dashes GREEN CRÈME DE MENTHE	1 dash ANGOSTURA BITTERS

Shake ice with gin, bitters, lemon juice and Crème de Menthe. Strain off into cocktail glass to serve.

(This differs from the New Zealander's Fallen Angel Cocktail, which consists of 2 msrs. Amsterdam in a glass, topped up with equal parts of lemonade and ginger ale.)

DELMONICO

2 msrs. GIN	2-3 dashes ANGOSTURA BITTERS
1 msr. BRANDY	slice of LEMON PEEL
1 msr. sweet ITALIAN VERMOUTH	ICE CUBES
1 msr. dry FRENCH VERMOUTH	

Add Angostura bitters to ice cubes in mixing glass and stir in gin, brandy and both vermouths. Strain off into chilled glass, adding a twist of lemon before serving.

LUIGI

2 msrs. GIN	1 teaspoon GRENADINE
1 msr. FRENCH VERMOUTH	1 msr. ORANGE JUICE
½ msr. COINTREAU	ICE CUBES

Pour gin, vermouth, Cointreau, Grenadine and orange juice over ice in mixing glass. Stir, and strain off into a chilled glass and serve.

ALASKA

When she first mentioned the North West Passage, I took her for a medical student.

And when she said she studied the way other people lived, I thought she must be a gossip columnist.

Months later, living like Eskimos in the Arctic, she suggested we set up home together. Luckily I had a *Build Yourself An Igloo* manual handy.

While I struggled with the ice cubes, she rustled up something with gin. She called it Alaska.

We huddled together for warmth. After a while, she unbottoned her fur and moved closer.

"Anthropology is all very fine," she whispered, "but have you ever wondered what Eskimos do *after* they've rubbed noses?"

CLOVER CLUB COCKTAIL

1½ msrs. DRY GIN	juice of ½ LEMON
4 dashes GRENADINE	white of 1 EGG
CRACKED ICE	

Shake ice with gin, lemon juice, egg white and Grenadine. Pour into champagne glass and serve.

CORONATION COCKTAIL

½ msr. DRY GIN	½ msr. DUBONNET
CRACKED ICE.	½ msr. FRENCH VERMOUTH

Stir ice with gin, vermouth and Dubonnet. Strain into cocktail glass, and serve immediately.

Left to right: Clover Club, Coronation, Bronx, Blue Moon.

BRONX COCKTAIL

1 msr. DRY GIN	1 dash FRENCH VERMOUTH
½ msr. ORANGE JUICE	1 dash ITALIAN VERMOUTH
CRACKED ICE	

Shake ice with gin, orange juice and both vermouths. Serve in cocktail glass.

BLUE MOON COCKTAIL

1 msr. DRY GIN	½ msr. CRÈME YVETTE
½ msr. LEMON JUICE	CRACKED ICE

Stir ice with gin, lemon juice and Crème Yvette. Strain off into cocktail glass to serve.

PINK GIN

1½ msrs. GIN	3 dashes ANGOSTURA BITTERS
1 msr. WATER	2 CUBES ICE

Put dashes of bitters in goblet, and rotate. Throw out the bitters and put ice cubes in goblet. Add gin and water and serve.

PERFECT COCKTAIL

1½ msrs. DRY GIN	¾ msr. SWEET VERMOUTH
¾ msr. DRY VERMOUTH	

Stir together gin and both vermouths. Pour, and serve immediately in cocktail glass.

NEW YORKER COCKTAIL

½ msr. GIN	1 dash COINTREAU
½ msr. DRY SHERRY	CRACKED ICE
1½ msrs. FRENCH VERMOUTH	

Stir ice with gin, vermouth, sherry and Cointreau. Present and serve in cocktail glass.

Left to right: Pink Gin, Perfect, New Yorker, Orange Blossom.

ORANGE BLOSSOM COCKTAIL

1 msr. GIN	CRACKED ICE
2 msrs. ORANGE JUICE	

Shake ice with gin and orange. Strain off into cocktail glass and serve immediately.

MAIDEN'S PRAYER

2 msrs. GIN	juice of 1 LEMON
1 msr. COINTREAU	ICE CUBES
3 drops ANGOSTURA BITTERS	

Shake ice with all ingredients until mixture becomes frosty. Strain off and serve in a sour glass.

MONKEY'S GLAND

2 msrs. GIN	1 msr. ORANGE JUICE
½ teaspoon GRENADINE	ICE CUBES
3 dashes PERNOD	

Add all ingredients to ice in mixing glass. Stir and strain off to serve in a chilled martini glass.

BLÉRIOT

Learning to fly is easier than you might think.

First, take the joystick in both hands.

Spin the prop and check for vibrations. Make sure the wings are fully extended.

You are now ready for takeoff.

Apply the throttle, ease down the runway, pull back into a vertical climb.

After that the clouds are yours for the taking. Just as they were for Louis Blériot.

One thing, though. Beware of excessive turbulence.

It can play havoc with your undercarriage.

SAN FRANCISCO

1½ msrs. SLOE GIN	1 dash ORANGE BITTERS
¼ msr. SWEET VERMOUTH	1 MARASCHINO CHERRY
¼ msr. DRY VERMOUTH	ICE
1 dash ANGOSTURA BITTERS	

In mixing glass stir ice with gin, both vermouths and orange and Angostura bitters. Add cherry and serve in cocktail glass.

ROLLS ROYCE

1 msr. GIN	½ msr. SWEET VERMOUTH
¼ msr. BENEDICTINE	CRACKED ICE
½ msr. DRY VERMOUTH	

Stir ice with gin, both vermouths and Benedictine. Strain off into cocktail glass to serve.

QUEEN'S COCKTAIL

1 msr. DRY GIN	1 msr. SWEET VERMOUTH
1 msr. DRY VERMOUTH	1 MARASCHINO CHERRY
1 msr. PINEAPPLE JUICE	1 piece PINEAPPLE

Shake together gin, both vermouths and pineapple juice. Pour into cocktail glass, and add pineapple and cherry decor before serving.

Left to right: San Francisco, Rolls Royce, Queen's, Pink Lady.

PINK LADY

2 msrs. GIN	1 dash EGG WHITE
4 dashes GRENADINE	

Shake egg white with Grenadine and gin. Strain off into cocktail glass to serve.

WHITE LADY

1 msr. GIN	juice of ½ LEMON
½ msr. COINTREAU	dash of EGG WHITE

Shake together gin, Cointreau and lemon juice with egg white. Pour and serve in cocktail glass.

VIRGIN COCKTAIL

1 msr. DRY GIN	1 MARASCHINO CHERRY
¾ msr. CRÈME DE MENTHE	

Shake together gin and Crème de Menthe. Strain off into cocktail glass, and add cherry before serving.

SHERRY COCKTAIL

1 msr. GIN	1 msr. SWEET SHERRY
1 msr. LEMON JUICE	

Shake together gin and lemon juice and sherry. Strain off into cocktail glass to serve.

Left to right: White Lady, Virgin, Sherry, Negroni.

NEGRONI

1 msr. DRY GIN	SODA WATER
¾ msr. SWEET VERMOUTH	ICE
½ msr. CAMPARI BITTERS	LEMON PEEL

Stir ice with gin, bitters and vermouth in a mixing glass. Pour off into cocktail glass, add splash of soda water and lemon peel and serve.

NEW ORLEANS FIZZ

2 msrs. DRY GIN	white of 1 EGG
1 msr. SWEET CREAM	2-3 dashes ORANGE FLOWER WATER
1 msr. LEMON JUICE	1 dash VANILLA
1 teaspoon SUGAR	CRACKED ICE
SODA WATER	

Shake cracked ice with all ingredients excepting soda water, until mixture becomes frothy. Strain off into tall highball glass and top up with soda water to serve.

RAMOZ FIZZ

2 msrs. DRY GIN	2 dashes of ORANGE FLOWER WATER
1 msr. LEMON JUICE	1 teaspoon SUGAR
1 msr. LIME JUICE	1 EGG WHITE
1 msr. HEAVY CREAM	CRACKED ICE

Shake cracked ice with mixture of all ingredients. Frost the rim of 10oz highball glass with lemon and sugar (see Crustas, Page 109), strain into this prepared glass and serve.

FALLEN ANGEL

There comes a time when all angels must fall.

It's just a question of when and where, and of whom gets the pleasure of finally unfastening those wings.

A word of warning to angel hunters, though.

As the poppers pop and those silken wings slide to the ground, you may find that your fallen angel can still fly you to the corners of the Universe.

In which case, mix yourself another delicious cocktail.

And drink to your good fortune.

SWAN

2 msrs. GIN	3 dashes PERNOD
1 msr. FRENCH VERMOUTH	juice of FRESH LIME
2 dashes ANGOSTURA BITTERS	ICE CUBES

Pour lime juice over ice in mixing glass, followed by Pernod and Angostura bitters. Add vermouth and gin, stir well and strain off to serve in chilled glass.

WHITE ELEPHANT

3 msrs. GIN	white of 1 EGG
1 msr. sweet ITALIAN VERMOUTH	ICE CUBES

Shake ice with all ingredients until mixture becomes frosty. Strain off and serve in a sour glass.

VIRGIN

2 msrs. GIN	1 msr. FORBIDDEN FRUIT
1 msr. CRÈME DE MENTHE	ICE CUBES

Shake ice with all ingredients until mixture becomes frosty. Strain off and serve in a sour glass.

ROLLS ROYCE

She moves like a wraith, gliding silently down country lanes.

You sink into that soft leather and savour the journey ahead.

The chauffeur's head never turns.

The only sound is the ticking of the clock. And perhaps the occasional pop of a cork. Or of a suspender.

At last, you stretch forward and mix yourself another long smooth drink, and reflect that this really is the only way to get from A to B.

Entwined. In luxury. Every single inch of the way.

BLACK
Highland Malt

Whatever might be the merits of one whisky (or whiskey) over another it's seldom disputed that Scotch has an individuality that's hard to beat, if not to swallow. The soft spring waters of Scotland are said to contribute much to the unique quality of that country's variety of a drink which derives its name from the Gaelic 'uisge beatha', phonetically pronounced "whisky", and meaning 'water of life'.

Scotch whisky is a blend of Scotch malt and Scotch grain whiskies. It was the early Scottish settlers who took their distilling knowledge with them to the New World and produced Canadian Whisky. Because they added rye to the grain mixture, it's often called Canadian rye.

Irish whiskey is produced from a mash of cereal grains, and after a different distilling process to that used in the production of Scotch, it's left to age for upwards of five years before use.

The first production of American Bourbon whiskey is accredited to the Rev. Elijah Craig. In 1789 the Baptist minister set up a still at Bourbon and made Kentucky Bourbon whiskey, a spirit now defined basically as that produced from a mash comprising of not less than 51% grain. Other types of whisky (or whiskey) produced in other parts of the world generally owe their individuality mostly to local crop and climatic conditions, and possible variances in maturation procedures.

Although some cocktail recipes may recommend the use of one particular type of whisky (or whiskey) or another, there's nothing against trying straightforward Scotch in any of them if some less common varieties are not at hand.

MANHATTAN (dry)

1½ msrs. CANADIAN WHISKY	1 or 2 (optional) dashes ANGOSTURA BITTERS
¾ msr. DRY VERMOUTH	
OLIVE or LEMON TWIST	ICE

Stir ice with whisky, vermouth and bitters and strain contents off to serve in cocktail glass. Add olive or lemon twist before serving.

MANHATTAN (sweet)

¾ msr. SWEET VERMOUTH	MARASCHINO CHERRY

Similar to dry (above), but substituting sweet vermouth for dry and a Maraschino cherry for the olive or lemon twist. Angostura dash still optional, but try limiting to a single.

MAMIE TAYLOR

2 msrs. SCOTCH WHISKY	GINGER ALE
ICE	LEMON SLICE

Pour Scotch into glass containing ice and top up with ginger ale. Add slice of lemon before serving.

LEPRECHAUN DANCER

2 msrs. IRISH WHISKEY	ICE
2 msrs. LEMON JUICE	DRY GINGER ALE
SODA WATER	LEMON PEEL

Pour whiskey and lemon juice into glass containing ice. Top up with equal parts of soda water and ginger ale. Place twist of lemon in glass and serve.

Left to right: Manhattan (dry), Mamie Taylor, Manhattan (sweet), Leprechaun Dancer.

MORNING GLORY

1½ msrs. SCOTCH WHISKY	ICE
1 teaspoon CASTOR SUGAR	SODA WATER
WHITE OF EGG	

Shake Scotch, egg white and sugar and strain off into glass containing ice. Top up with soda water before serving.

NEW YORK COCKTAIL

2 msrs. CANADIAN WHISKY	juice of ½ LEMON
4 dashes GRENADINE	ICE
ORANGE PEEL	

Shake ice with Grenadine, whisky and lemon juice. Strain off into cocktail glass. Decorate with orange peel twist before serving.

RUSTY NAIL

1½ msrs. DRAMBUIE	ICE
1½ msrs. SCOTCH WHISKY	LEMON PEEL

Pour Scotch and Drambuie onto ice in old-fashioned glass. Add lemon peel twist and serve.

Left to right: Morning Glory, New York, Rusty Nail, Rob Roy.

ROB ROY

½ msr. SCOTCH WHISKY	ICE
½ msr. SWEET VERMOUTH	MARASCHINO CHERRY
1 dash ANGOSTURA BITTERS	

Stir Scotch, vermouth and bitters with ice in mixing glass. Pour into cocktail glass, add cherry and serve.

BLUE BLAZER

2 msrs. SCOTCH WHISKY	LEMON PEEL
2 msrs. BOILING WATER	2 MUGS
SUGAR	

Pour whisky into one silver, or copper mug and fill other with boiling water. Set light to whisky, and whilst burning mix ingredients together by repetitively pouring from one mug to another, about five times. Add sugar to taste. Decorate with lemon peel before serving.

CARLTON COCKTAIL

1 msr. CANADIAN WHISKY	½ msr. COINTREAU
½ msr. ORANGE JUICE	CRACKED ICE

Shake cracked ice, whisky, orange juice and Cointreau. Strain into cocktail glass and serve.

BOOMERANG

In the outback you should always take a curvy friend with you.

Namely, your boomerang.

It will take great care of you, no matter how protracted your walkabout.

A word to the wise, though. Be careful who you allow to use your boomerang.

Some people won't know how to handle. Others will never have seen one before.

So take our advice. Mix her a dinkum cocktail and explain, very carefully, exactly what it's for.

She'll be enthralled.

And you'll find that, just like your boomerang, she will soon come back for more.

SCOTCH MIST

2 msrs. SCOTCH WHISKY	LEMON PEEL
ICE	

Shake whisky with crushed ice. Pour unstrained into old-fashioned glass, add lemon twist and serve.

TENNESSEE SNIFTER

TENNESSEE WHISKEY

Pour warm water over brandy balloon to heat glass. Dry glass and pour in three measures of Tennessee whiskey, and sip enjoyably.

TENNESSEE SOUR

2 msrs. TENNESSEE WHISKEY	SODA WATER
juice of ½ LEMON	MARASCHINO CHERRY
ICE	½ slice ORANGE

Shake ice with lemon juice, whiskey and sugar. Strain into sour glass and top up with soda water. Decorate with orange and cherry before serving.

TENNESSEE MANHATTAN (dry)

1½ msrs. TENNESSEE WHISKEY	ICE
¾ msr. DRY VERMOUTH	OLIVE or LEMON TWIST
1 or 2 dashes ANGOSTURA BITTERS	

Stir ice with whiskey, vermouth and bitters. Strain into cocktail glass, add olive or the lemon twist and serve.

Left to right: Scotch Mist, Tennessee Snifter, Tennessee Sour, Tennessee Manhattan (dry).

BOILERMAKER

1½-2 msrs. SCOTCH WHISKY	BEER

Scotch is served straight, with glass of beer as chaser.

BOOMERANG COCKTAIL

1 msr. CANADIAN WHISKY	2 dashes LEMON JUICE
¾ msr. DRY VERMOUTH	ICE
¾ msr. SWEDISH PUNCH	

Shake ice with whisky, vermouth, punch and lemon juice. Strain into cocktail glass and serve.

Left to right: Boilermaker, Boomerang, Bobby Burns, Whiz Bang.

BOBBY BURNS

½ msr. SCOTCH WHISKY	1 dash BENEDICTINE
¼ msr. DRY VERMOUTH	ICE CUBES
¼ msr. SWEET VERMOUTH	LEMON PEEL

Mix Scotch, Benedictine and vermouths by stirring in with ice. Serve in cocktail glass after topping with lemon peel twist.

WHIZ BANG

3 msrs. WHISKY	2-3 dashes ORANGE BITTERS
1 msr. dry FRENCH VERMOUTH	½ teaspoon CRÈME DE MENTHE
½ teaspoon GRENADINE	ICE CUBES

Add orange bitters to ice in mixing glass. Pour in whisky, vermouth and Grenadine and stir well. Strain off into a chilled martini glass, adding Crème de Menthe before serving.

EDINBURGH

3 msrs. WHISKY	2-3 dashes ANGOSTURA BITTERS
1 msr. dry FRENCH VERMOUTH	½ teaspoon APRICOT BRANDY
½ teaspoon CRÈME DE MENTHE	ICE CUBES

Place ice cubes in mixing glass, adding bitters, brandy and Crème de Menthe. Pour in whisky and vermouth, and stir vigorously. Strain off into a chilled martini glass, and serve.

HARRITY

3 msrs. SCOTCH (or BOURBON)	3 dashes ANGOSTURA BITTERS
1 msr. GIN	ICE CUBES

Splash Angostura bitters over ice in mixing glass. Add Pernod, vermouth and Scotch (or Bourbon). Stir well, strain off and serve in a chilled martini glass.

MAPLE LEAF

Next time you meet a pretty girl in a hotel corridor, wearing nothing but a maple leaf, don't jump to conclusions.

"You're Canadian," I said admiringly, flexing my knowledge of flags.

"Not at all," she blushed. "I'm a librarian."

"It doesn't show," I said.

"I've just come back from a Fancy Dress party and I've lost my key. Can you help me?"

"Of course," I smiled. "Come and hide yourself in my room. I'll mix us a couple of Maple Leaves and then . . . "

"And then?"

"Well, we'll just settle down and wait for Autumn."

WARD 8

1½ msrs. CANADIAN WHISKY	1 msr. LEMON JUICE
¼ msr. GRENADINE	½ teaspoon POWDERED SUGAR
CRACKED ICE	DECORATIVE FRUITS

Shake cracked ice with whisky, Grenadine, lemon juice and sugar. Strain off into cocktail glass and decorate with fruit. Serve with a drinking straw.

Left to right: Ward 8, Ward Eight, Bourbon Mint Julep, Whisky Cobbler.

WARD EIGHT
(alternative to above)

1½ msrs. RYE WHISKEY	CRACKED ICE
½ msr. LEMON JUICE	1 teaspoon GRENADINE
½ msr. ORANGE JUICE	

Shake cracked ice with whiskey, Grenadine and orange and lemon juices. To serve, strain off into cocktail glass.

BOURBON MINT JULEP

2 msrs. BOURBON	1 dash DARK RUM or BRANDY
½ teaspoon SUGAR	Decorative MINT, LEMON and CHERRY
4 sprigs MINT	
CRACKED ICE	

Mix Bourbon, mint and sugar and stir into glass of cracked ice. Stir until outside of glass becomes frosted and then top with dash of brandy or dark rum. Add decorative sprig of mint, lemon or a cherry, and serve with straws.

WHISKY COBBLER

2 msrs. SCOTCH WHISKY	1 LEMON SLICE
4 dashes CURAÇAO	MINT SPRIG
4 dashes BRANDY	DECOROUS FRUIT
ICE	

Fill goblet with cracked ice. Stir in Scotch, curaçao, brandy and slice of lemon. Decorate with mint and fruit before serving.

OLD-FASHIONED

1 msr. WHISKY	1 cube SUGAR
2 dashes ANGOSTURA BITTERS	slice of LEMON PEEL
ICE CUBES	1 MARASCHINO CHERRY

Stir in Angostura bitters to dissolve sugar cube in bottom of old-fashioned glass. Add ice cubes and pour in whisky. Twist lemon peel over drink, drop it in, and garnish with cherry to serve.

BLINKER COCKTAIL

½ msr. CANADIAN WHISKY	¼ msr. GRENADINE
¾ msr. GRAPEFRUIT JUICE	CRACKED ICE

Shake ice with whisky, grapefruit juice and Grenadine. Serve in chilled cocktail glass.

ADAM AND EVE

1 lump SUGAR	3 cubes ICE
1 dash BITTERS	2 msrs. TENNESSEE WHISKEY
SODA WATER	½ msr. GALLIANO

Add sufficient soda to cover sugar and bitters placed in old-fashioned glass and stir well. Add ice cubes and pour in whiskey, before floating Galliano on top. Ready to serve.

Left to right: Old-Fashioned, Blinker, Adam and Eve, Bessie and Jessie.

BESSIE AND JESSIE

2 msrs. AMERICAN BLENDED WHISKEY	1 msr. ADVOKAAT
6 msrs. MILK	ICE

Shake ice with whiskey and milk and pour into highball glass. Gently pour Advokaat on top and serve.

MAPLE LEAF

⅓ msr. BOURBON	1 teaspoon MAPLE SYRUP
⅓ msr. LIME JUICE	CRACKED ICE

Shake ice with Bourbon, lemon juice and syrup and strain off into glass to serve.

ALGONQUIN

3 msrs. SCOTCH (or BOURBON)	1 msr. unsweetened PINEAPPLE JUICE
1 msr. dry FRENCH VERMOUTH	
ICE CUBES	

Stir ice cubes with all ingredients in mixing glass very briskly until mixture is almost frothy. Strain off and serve in a chilled martini glass.

STONE

2 msrs. WHISKY	ICE CUBES
CIDER	

Add whisky to ice cubes in a highball glass, and top up with cider. Stir well before serving.

BORDEN

3 msrs. WHISKY	3 dashes PERNOD
1 msr. sweet ITALIAN VERMOUTH	ICE CUBES
2 dashes ANGOSTURA BITTERS	

Add Angostura bitters and Pernod to ice cubes in mixing glass. Pour in whisky and vermouth. Stir, and strain off into a chilled martini glass to serve.

Left to right: Maple Leaf, Algonquin, Stone, Borden.

FRENCH 95

See French 75 under Gin Cocktails and substitute Bourbon Whiskey for gin ingredient.

EDWARD VIII COCKTAIL

1½ msrs. CANADIAN WHISKY	2 teaspoons ITALIAN VERMOUTH
1 dash PERNOD	ICE
2 teaspoons WATER	1 piece ORANGE PEEL

Stir ice with whisky, vermouth, water and orange peel, and it's ready to serve in an old-fashioned glass.

IRISH ON THE ROCKS

Simply pour 1½ msrs. of Irish whiskey into glass of ice and serve.

Left to right: French 95, Edward VIII, Irish on the Rocks, Deshler.

DESHLER COCKTAIL

¾ msr. CANADIAN WHISKY	1 strip LEMON PEEL
¾ msr. DUBONNET	1 strip ORANGE PEEL
2 dashes COINTREAU	CRACKED ICE
2 dashes BITTERS	

Shake cracked ice with whisky, Cointreau, Dubonnet and bitters. Strain into pre-chilled cocktail glass. Twist lemon and orange peels onto drink before serving.

Vodka has been a popular type of drink in Russia and Poland ever since the 1100's when it was the generic term for a spirit drink of any kind produced from the distillation of any type of grain, grape or even potato, and to which strong flavourings and aromatics had been added.

A state monopoly had to be established in Russia during the mid-1920's for the production of vodka in order to control what had become a thriving black market trade.

However, refugees from the Russian Revolution set up stills in new homelands to which they had fled, and continued to produce vodka. The major difference was that these 'western' vodkas as the drinks became known, were completely without any additive flavourings.

Although this flavourless vodka provided a wonderfully neutral base spirit for use in mixed drink receipes it was not until the 1940's that vodka became accepted as a popular and fashionable drink in the West. Flavoured vodkas are still available in some parts of Europe where, by custom, they are chilled and then drunk neat.

SCREWDRIVER

1½ msrs. VODKA	2 cubes ICE
ORANGE JUICE	slice of ORANGE
1 MARASCHINO CHERRY	

Pour vodka over ice cubes placed in highball glass. Fill up with orange juice, top with cherry and slice of orange and it's ready to serve.

Left to right: Screwdriver, Vodka Martini, Salty Dog, Russian.

VODKA MARTINI

Same recipe as for Gin Martini, but using vodka in place of gin. (See Page 32).

SALTY DOG

1½ msrs. VODKA	3 cubes ICE
GRAPEFRUIT JUICE	

Add vodka to ice cubes already placed in glass. Fill up with grapefruit juice to serve.

RUSSIAN COCKTAIL

1 msr. VODKA	1 msr. CRÈME DE CACAO
1 msr. DRY GIN	

Shake together gin, Crème de Cacao and vodka. Strain off into cocktail glass to serve.

MOSCOW MULE

2 msrs. VODKA	3 cubes ICE
1 msr. LEMON JUICE	MINT sprig for decor
GINGER BEER	

Place 3 ice cubes in glass, pour in vodka and lemon juice, and top up with ginger beer. Before serving, decorate with mint.

Left to right: Moscow Mule, Black Russian, Bloody Mary, Harvey Wallbanger.

BLACK RUSSIAN

3 msrs. VODKA	ICE
1 msr. KAHLUA	

Place ice in tall glass and pour in Kahlua and vodka.

BLOODY MARY

2 msrs. VODKA	SALT and PEPPER
¼ msr. LEMON JUICE	1 dash WORCESTERSHIRE SAUCE
2 drops TABASCO SAUCE	3 cubes ICE
TOMATO JUICE	

Place Worcestershire sauce, Tabasco sauce and lemon juice in glass, and add salt and pepper to taste. Mix together, adding in vodka and ice cubes. Top up with tomato juice, and serve with swizzle stick.
(White rum, gin or Tequila can be substituted for vodka).

HARVEY WALLBANGER

1 msr. VODKA	ORANGE JUICE
1 msr. GALLIANO	CHERRY and ORANGE slice for decor

Pour vodka and Galliano into glass and top up with orange juice. Add cherry and slice of orange to garnish before serving.

BIKINI

3 msrs. VODKA	1 teaspoon SUGAR
1 msr. WHITE RUM	juice of ½ LEMON
½ msr. MILK	CRACKED ICE

Add vodka, lemon juice, white rum, milk and sugar to ice in shaker. Shake until frosty, strain off and serve in a chosen glass.

HEAD-OVER-HEELS

3 msrs. VODKA	juice of 1 LEMON
3 dashes ANGOSTURA BITTERS	1 teaspoon SUGAR SYRUP
CHAMPAGNE	CRACKED ICE

Add vodka, sugar syrup, lemon (or lime) juice, and bitters to ice in shaker, and shake until frosty. Pour unstrained into a highball glass, and top up with champagne to serve.

AMELIA'S RIP CORD

2 msrs. VODKA	juice of ½ LEMON
1 msr. dry FRENCH VERMOUTH	juice of ½ small GRAPEFRUIT
¾ msr. COINTREAU	ICE CUBES

Pour vodka, vermouth, Cointreau and fruit juices over ice in mixing glass. Stir gently, pour into a chilled glass and serve.

AMELIA'S RIPCORD

Amelia came into my life right out of the blue. Literally.
There I was in the garden, taking turns with the cocktail shaker and the lawnmower, when she floated in, trailing a smoke canister.
Carefully, I unravelled her from my greenhouse. She was exhilarated and quite breathless.
"Gosh! I hope you don't mind me dropping in like this."
"Not at all," I said. "I'm never averse to a windfall as pretty as you are."
I shook up a new cocktail for her, there and then. I called it Amelia's Ripcord.
"Super," she said. "Actually, I always need a drink after a jump."
"That's quite a coincidence," I said, sipping at my cocktail. "I always need a drink before one."

JERRY'S JOY

⅓ msr. VODKA	1 dash ORANGE BITTERS
⅓ msr. LILLET	1 dash EGG WHITE
⅓ msr. COINTREAU	1 MARASCHINO CHERRY
CRACKED ICE	

Shake ice with vodka, Lillet, Cointreau, bitters and egg white. Strain off into glass and add cherry to serve.

(Quantities of Vodka, Lillet and Cointreau might vary slightly according to the strength of drink required but they must always remain in equal proportions of one-third each ingredient.)

UPSTAIRS

⅓ msr. VODKA	⅙ msr. LIME JUICE
⅓ msr. PORT WINE	CRACKED ICE
⅙ msr. LAKKA LIQUEUR	

Shake ice with vodka, port wine, liqueur and lime juice. Strain off into cocktail glass and serve immediately.

PRIZE IDIOT

1 msr. VODKA	1 dash GRENADINE
1 msr. CRÈME DE BANANE	1 GREEN CHERRY
2 dashes LEMON JUICE	slice of LEMON
FIZZY LEMON	CRACKED ICE

Add vodka, crème de banane, lemon juice and Grenadine to ice-filled highball glass and stir in fizz lemon as required. Decorate with the cherry and a lemon slice and serve with muddler and straws.

Left to right: Jerry's Joy, Upstairs, Prize Idiot.

VODKA ZAZA

2 msrs. VODKA	3 dashes ORANGE BITTERS
1 msr. DUBONNET	ICE CUBES

Splash bitters over ice in mixing glass and add vodka and Dubonnet. Stir the mixture well, and strain off to serve in a chilled martini glass. You can also try substituting Angostura for the orange bitters.

Left to right: Vodka Zaza, Opossum, Vodka Silver Fizz, Surf Rider.

OPOSSUM

3 msrs. VODKA	juice of ½ ORANGE
SODA WATER	½ teaspoon GRENADINE
3 dashes ANGOSTURA BITTERS	1 slice ORANGE
juice of 1 LEMON	CRACKED ICE

Pour vodka, fruit juices, bitters and Grenadine over ice in shaker. Shake until frosty. Pour unstrained into chosen glass. Top up with soda water, and garnish with orange to serve.

VODKA SILVER FIZZ

3 msrs. VODKA	½ teaspoon SUGAR SYRUP
SODA WATER	juice of 1 LEMON
white of 1 EGG	CRACKED ICE

Pour vodka, sugar syrup, lemon juice, and egg white over ice in shaker. Shake until frosty, and pour without straining directly into highball glass. Top up with soda water to serve.

SURF RIDER

3 msrs. VODKA	juice of ½ LEMON
1 msr. sweet ITALIAN VERMOUTH	juice of 1 ORANGE
½ teaspoon GRENADINE	CRACKED ICE

Pour vodka, vermouth, fruit juices and Grenadine over ice in shaker. Shake until frosty, and strain off to serve in a sour glass.

HERE'S HOW

1 msr. VODKA	white of 1 EGG
1 msr. PALE BRANDY	juice of 1 LEMON
½ teaspoon SUGAR SYRUP	CRACKED ICE

Pour vodka, brandy, lemon juice, sugar syrup and egg white over ice in shaker. Shake until frosty, and strain off to serve in a sour glass.

INSPIRATION

2 msrs. VODKA	1 slice LEMON PEEL
½ msr. BENEDICTINE	ICE CUBES
½ msr. dry FRENCH VERMOUTH	

Add vodka, Benedictine and vermouth to ice cubes in mixing glass. Stir well, and strain off to serve in a chilled martini glass.

CUPID'S BOW

As you may have noticed, darts is an up and coming sport.

But beware if you're asked to play by a girl who doesn't quite look the part.

Too pretty. Too skimpily dressed. Too cherubic by half.

You might find that your aim becomes none too steady. That even before you've hit your double, her arrows will already have hit home.

You'll feel weak at the knees. Even a one-hundred-and-eighty won't help you now.

Our advice to you is to get her a Cupid's Bow cocktail.

It won't nullify the effect of those arrows.

But it might, just, get you both into something of a quiver.

GODMOTHER

1½ msrs. VODKA	ICE
¾ msr. AMARETTO	

Fill up old-fashioned glass with ice and gently add the vodka and the amaretto to serve.

CHI CHI

1½ msrs. VODKA	1 MARASCHINO CHERRY
1 msr. COCONUT CREAM	slice of PINEAPPLE
4 msrs. non-sweet PINEAPPLE JUICE	CRACKED or CRUSHED ICE

This is a blended drink and best mixed in an electric liquidizer. Place cracked ice in liquidizer adding vodka, coconut cream and pineapple juice. Keep blending time short, otherwise you'll get a very diluted drink. Strain off into large glass and decorate with cherry and pineapple slice before serving with straws.

Left to right: Godmother, Chi Chi, Vodka Mist, Bullshot.

VODKA MIST

1½ msrs. VODKA	twist of LEMON

Shake vodka with twist of lemon and serve unstrained in old-fashioned glass.

BULLSHOT

1-1½ msrs. VODKA	LEMON PEEL
2 msrs. HOT WATER	1 cube BEEF STOCK
FRESH LEMON	¼ tablespoon SALT
ICE	

Dissolve stock cube in hot water, adding salt, a squeeze of lemon and vodka. Stir ingredients briskly and serve on rocks in old-fashioned glass, after garnishing with lemon peel.

(In the above recipe, rum may be substituted for vodka and celery salt for salt).

SEAFOAM

3 msrs. VODKA	juice of 1 LIME
½ teaspoon SUGAR	CRACKED ICE
white of 1 EGG	

Pour vodka, fruit juice, egg white and sugar over ice in shaker. Shake until frosty, and strain off to serve in a sour glass.

HAVEN

1 msr. VODKA	3 dashes GRENADINE
1 msr. PERNOD	ICE CUBES

Splash the Grenadine over ice cubes in old-fashioned glass and add vodka and Pernod. Stir gently before serving.

PERTH

3 msrs. VODKA	juice of 1 LEMON
1 msr. sweet ITALIAN VERMOUTH	ICE CUBES
½ teaspoon GRENADINE	

Pour vodka, vermouth, lemon juice and Grenadine over ice cubes in mixing glass and stir gently. Strain off to serve in a chilled martini glass.

Left to right: Seafoam, Haven, Perth, Banjo.

BANJO

3 msrs. VODKA	1 teaspoon SUGAR
1 msr. PINEAPPLE JUICE	1 MARASCHINO CHERRY
juice of ½ GRAPEFRUIT	CRACKED ICE

Pour vodka, sugar syrup, and fruit juices over ice in shaker. Shake until frosty. Strain into a sour glass, and add cherry to serve.

MAIDEN

2 msrs. VODKA	1 msr. FORBIDDEN FRUIT
1 msr. WHITE CRÈME DE MENTHE	CRACKED ICE

Add vodka, Crème de Menthe and Forbidden Fruit to ice in shaker. Shake until frosty, and strain off to serve in a chilled martini glass.

LA DAME BLANCHE

1 msr. VODKA	4-5 ICE CUBES
3 msrs. dry WHITE WINE	

Pour vodka and wine over ice cubes in mixing glass. Stir vigorously, strain off, and pour into a chilled glass.

LA DAME BLANCHE

Her Mercedes was pure white, inside and out.

Conveniently, it snowed all the way to her home. In Whitefriars, of course.

The apartment was a glistening white from end to end. White walls. White floors. A white-framed mirror by the window.

Even her cat was white. Which surprised me. I'd never seen a white leopard before.

Calmly I reached for the vodka and mixed her a drink. "La Dame Blanche," I said with a nod.

She game me a white smile. So did the leopard. Then she laughed softly, slipped out of her dress and went to the window.

"If you watch for just a moment," she said, "the White Lady is about to reveal a very dark secret."

Brandy is the generic term for this ardent spirit which is distilled only from the grape, and many different types are produced in wine-making countries throughout the world.

French brandies are considered to be among the finest. One of that country's most famous types derives its name from Cognac, the city situated in the Charente district where the grapes used in production are grown, fermented and distilled.

Armagnac, in the south-west, is another French region famous for the production of its own particular type of brandy.

Brandies, or cognacs, are ideally matured in casks made from oak which has been weathered to remove from the wood any excess tannin which could adversely affect the spirit. Subject to periodic checks of one sort or another the spirit remains encased until reaching maturity.

The age of maturity varies from the eighteen months to two years period required by the youngest French brandy, to a period of two to eight years necessary for any of the finer types.

The more mature a brandy is, the more costly it becomes to buy, and (some would argue!) is much too good to waste in a mixed drink. Unless a recipe prescribes otherwise it's advisable to use younger and less expensive brandies in any mixed drink.

Any brandy produced from fruit other than the grape — cherry or apricot for example — is often used in the composition of mixed drinks. They are generally referred to as 'fruit brandies'.

PARIS

3 msrs. BRANDY	5 dashes PERNOD
1 msr. dry FRENCH VERMOUTH	ICE CUBES

Add brandy, vermouth and Pernod to ice cubes in mixing glass. Stir well, and strain off to serve in a chilled martini glass.

Left to right: Paris, Balmoral, Fioupe, Mary Stuart.

BALMORAL

3 msrs. BRANDY	3 dashes ANGOSTURA BITTERS
1 msr. dry FRENCH VERMOUTH	ICE CUBES

Add the rum, vermouth and bitters to ice in mixing glass. Stir well, and strain off to serve in a chilled martini glass.

FIOUPE

3 msrs. BRANDY	1 slice LEMON PEEL
1 msr. BENEDICTINE	ICE CUBES
1 msr. dry FRENCH VERMOUTH	

Add brandy, vermouth and Benedictine to ice cubes in mixing glass. Stir well, strain off into a chilled martini glass and add lemon twist before serving.

MARY STUART

3 msrs. BRANDY	1 slice LEMON PEEL
1 msr. DRAMBUIE	ICE CUBES

Add brandy and Drambuie to ice in mixing glass. Stir well, strain off into a chilled martini glass and add lemon twist before serving.

CARNIVAL

⅓ msr. BRANDY	1 dash ORANGE JUICE
⅓ msr. APRICOT BRANDY	1 dash KIRSCH
⅓ msr. LILLET	CRACKED ICE

Shake ice with brandy, apricot brandy, Lillet, orange juice and kirsch before straining to serve in cocktail glass.

CORPSE REVIVER

1 msr. BRANDY	twist of LEMON
½ msr. CALVADOS	CRACKED ICE
½ msr. SWEET VERMOUTH	

Put ice in mixing glass and pour in brandy, sweet vermouth and calvados. Stir until cold and strain into cocktail glass.

CHERRY BLOSSOM

½ msr. BRANDY	1 dash GRENADINE
¾ msr. CHERRY BRANDY	1 dash CURAÇAO
1 dash LEMON JUICE	CRACKED ICE

Shake ice with all ingredients and strain off into cocktail glass to serve.

Left to right: Carnival, Corpse Reviver, Cherry Blossom, Fixer.

FIXER

½ msr. BRANDY	⅛ msr. CREAM
¼ msr. CRÈME DE NOYEAU	CRACKED ICE
⅛ msr. PRUNELLE	

Shake ice with all ingredients together and strain off into cocktail glass to serve.

EGG SOUR

1 msr. BRANDY	CRACKED ICE
1 msr. WHITE CURAÇAO	1 tablespoon CASTOR SUGAR
juice of ¼ LEMON	1 whole EGG

Shake cracked ice with brandy, egg, castor sugar, lemon juice and curaçao, before straining into sour glass to serve.

FRENCH 125

See French 75 under Gin Cocktails and substitute brandy for gin ingredient.

BETWEEN THE SHEETS

She weakened perceptibly as she caught sight of the satin sheets.

"I've never been able to resist satin," she giggled, bright eyed, as she slid silkily out of her dress.

"But darling, you . . . "

She waved my protests aside. Moments later, with her clothes in a neat pile at my feet, she slipped tantalisingly between the sheets.

My eyes searched desperately for some brandy and a cocktail shaker.

Then the assistant came over. He looked at her for a few moments, but his expression didn't change.

Finally he said: "May I say that the satin complements madam's skin tone perfectly."

After forty years at the department store, I suppose nothing surprised him any more.

MELBOURNE

3 msrs. BRANDY	1 slice LEMON PEEL
1 msr. CURAÇAO	ICE CUBES

Add brandy and curaçao to ice in mixing glass, and stir vigorously. Strain off to serve in a martini glass, adding lemon twist.

MORNING

3 msrs. BRANDY	½ teaspoon MARASCHINO
1 msr. CURAÇAO	½ teaspoon dry FRENCH VERMOUTH
5 dashes PERNOD	ICE CUBES
3 dashes ORANGE BITTERS	

Splash bitters over ice in mixing glass and add Pernod. Stir in the brandy, curaçao, Maraschino and vermouth. Strain off to serve in a chilled martini glass.
(If you fancy experimenting, try substituting Angostura for orange bitters and Grenadine for the Maraschino.)

FASCINATOR

2 msrs. BRANDY	½ teaspoon GRENADINE
1 msr. GIN	ICE CUBES
½ teaspoon WHITE CRÈME DE MENTHE	

Pour brandy, gin, Crème de Menthe and Grenadine over ice cubes in mixing glass. Stir well, and strain off to serve in a chilled martini glass.

ST. KITTS

3 msrs. BRANDY	1 MARASCHINO CHERRY
1 msr. dry FRENCH VERMOUTH	CRACKED ICE
juice of ½ GRAPEFRUIT	

Pour brandy, vermouth and grapefruit juice over ice in shaker. Shake until frosty. Strain off and top with cherry to serve in a chilled martini glass.

Left to right: Melbourne, Morning, Fascinator, St Kitts.

MONTY ROSA

3 msrs. BRANDY	juice of ½ LEMON
1 msr. COINTREAU	ICE CUBES

Stir ice vigorously with brandy, fruit juice and Cointreau in mixing glass. Strain off to serve in a chilled martini glass. You can try substituting lime juice for the lemon.

Left to right: Monty Rosa, Depth Bomb, Esquire, Burnt Orange.

DEPTH BOMB

2 msrs. BRANDY	juice of LEMON
1 msr. APPLE BRANDY	ICE CUBES
½ teaspoon GRENADINE	

Stir ice vigorously with brandy, lemon juice, Grenadine and Apple Brandy in mixing glass, straining off to serve in a chilled martini glass:

ESQUIRE

2 msrs. BRANDY	3 dashes ANGOSTURA BITTERS
1 msr. GIN	ICE CUBES

Splash bitters over ice in mixing glass and stir in brandy and gin. Strain off, and serve in a chilled martini glass.

BURNT ORANGE

3 msrs. BRANDY	juice of ½ ORANGE
3 dashes ORANGE or ANGOSTURA BITTERS	ICE CUBES

Splash bitters over ice in mixing glass, and stir in brandy and orange juice. Strain off to serve in chilled martini glass.

KLONDIKE

3 msrs. APPLE BRANDY	3 dashes ORANGE BITTERS
1 msr. dry FRENCH VERMOUTH	ICE CUBES

Splash bitters onto ice cubes in mixing glass, adding Apple Brandy and vermouth. Stir well and strain off to serve in a chilled martini glass.

THE PRINCE

3 msrs. BRANDY	½ teaspoon WHITE CRÈME DE MENTHE
3 dashes ORANGE or ANGOSTURA BITTERS	ICE CUBES
1 teaspoon SUGAR	

Splash bitters over ice in mixing glass and stir in brandy and sugar. Do not strain, but pour directly into an old fashioned glass, adding the white Crème de Menthe to the mixture before serving.

BOSOM CARESSER

It's always advisable to wrap up well.
Especially when you're liable to pop out at any time.
What better than a fur — mink, of course — to protect your assets and caress those valuable curves.
A fur will fondle you gently and handle you with care.
It will protect you from the icy grip of winter.
What's more, like this brandy-based cocktail, it will warm the heart of any man lucky enough to see you.

LEVIATHAN COCKTAIL

½ msr. BRANDY	¼ msr. ORANGE JUICE
¼ msr. SWEET VERMOUTH	ICE

Shake ice with vermouth, brandy and orange juice. Serve in cocktail glass.

SIDECAR

¼ msr. COINTREAU	¼ msr. LEMON JUICE
½ msr. BRANDY	ICE

Shake ice with Cointreau, brandy and lemon juice. Strain and serve in cocktail glass.

Left to right: Leviathan, Sidecar, Stinger, Jack in the Box.

STINGER

⅔ msr. BRANDY	ICE
⅓ msr. CRÈME DE MENTHE	

Use mixing glass to mix ice with brandy and Crème de Menthe. Serve in cocktail glass.

JACK-IN-THE-BOX

½ msr. PINEAPPLE JUICE	1 dash ANGOSTURA BITTERS
½ msr. APPLEJACK BRANDY	ICE

Shake ice with brandy, pineapple juice and bitters. Serve in cocktail glass.

FRENCH CONNECTION

1½ msrs. BRANDY	CRACKED ICE
1½ msrs. AMARETTO	

Put ice into glass in which drink is to be served, adding ingredients without any pre-mixing and serve with muddler.

MILLIONAIRE

¾ msr. BRANDY	⅛ msr. ORANGE CURAÇAO
⅛ msr. CRÈME DE NOYEAU	2 dashes ANGOSTURA BITTERS
⅛ msr. ORGEAT SYRUP	CRACKED ICE

Shake ice with all ingredients and strain into cocktail glass to serve.

Left to right: French Connection, Millionaire, Olympic, Red Hackle.

OLYMPIC

⅓ msr. BRANDY	⅓ msr. ORANGE JUICE
⅓ msr. ORANGE CURAÇAO	CRACKED ICE

Shake ice with all ingredients and strain into cocktail glass to serve.

RED HACKLE

½ msr. BRANDY	¼ msr. GRENADINE
¼ msr. DUBONNET	CRACKED ICE

Shake ice with brandy, Dubonnet and Grenadine and strain off into cocktail glass to serve.

THUNDER

3 msrs. BRANDY	yolk of 1 EGG
1 teaspoon SUGAR SYRUP	CRACKED ICE
GROUND BLACK PEPPER	

Pour brandy, egg yolk and sugar syrup over ice in shaker and sprinkle a little ground black pepper over the mixture. Shake until frosty. Strain off and serve.

TINKER

3 msrs. BRANDY	juice of ½ LEMON
DRY GINGER ALE	CRACKED ICE

Pour brandy and fruit juice over ice in shaker. Shake until frosty, and pour without straining directly into a highball glass. Top up with ginger ale to serve.

WHIP

¼ msr. BRANDY	¼ msr. CURAÇAO
¼ msr. PASTIS	CRACKED ICE
¼ msr. DRY VERMOUTH	

Shake ice with brandy, pastis, vermouth and curaçao and strain off into cocktail glass to serve.

JACK IN THE BOX

For the first time in your life you're happily settled down.

The TR6 has gone, and you're mortgaged up to the eyebrows and beyond.

On the whole, though, you're quite content.

Then, suddenly, at a party, one of your old flames pops up unexpectedly.

She's as beautiful as ever, and wearing one of those fetching little numbers of hers.

You mix her a drink — a Jack in the Box — and laugh warmly about old times.

She suggests a nightcap, but you're already running late. She smiles and plants a moist kiss on your cheek.

You drive home alone with your might-have-beens. And you reflect — sadly perhaps — that in life, not quite everything comes gift-wrapped.

BETWEEN THE SHEETS

¾ msr. RUM	ICE
¾ msr. TRIPLE SEC	juice of ½ LEMON
¾ msr. BRANDY	

Shake ice with rum, triple sec, brandy and lemon juice. Strain off to serve into cocktail glass.

BOMBAY COCKTAIL

2 msrs. BRANDY	ICE
¼ msr. DRY VERMOUTH	3 dashes CURAÇAO
¼ msr. SWEET VERMOUTH	

Shake ice with curaçao, both vermouths and brandy. Strain off ready to serve into cocktail glass.

Left to right: Between the Sheets, Bombay, B & B, American Beauty.

B & B

½ msr. BRANDY	½ msr. BENEDICTINE

Pour Benedictine into liqueur glass, add brandy and serve.

AMERICAN BEAUTY COCKTAIL

½ msr. BRANDY	½ msr. GRENADINE
½ msr. DRY VERMOUTH	½ msr. ORANGE JUICE
3 dashes WHITE CRÈME DE MENTHE	PORT WINE
ICE	

Shake ice with brandy, dry vermouth, Crème de Menthe, Grenadine and orange juice. Strain off into cocktail glass, top up with port wine, and serve.

BRANDY ALEXANDER

⅓ msr. BRANDY	⅓ FRESH CREAM
⅓ msr. CRÈME DE CACAO	NUTMEG

Shake ice with fresh cream, brandy and Crème de Cacao. Strain off into champagne glass. Sprinkle nutmeg on top before serving.

COFFEE COCKTAIL

1 msr. BRANDY	dash of CURAÇAO
1 msr. PORT WINE	yolk of 1 EGG
1 teaspoon SUGAR	ICE
NUTMEG	

Shake with ice, the brandy, curaçao, sugar, egg yolk and port wine. Strain into glass, sprinkle nutmeg on top and serve.

DEVIL COCKTAIL

1⅓ msr. BRANDY	1⅓ msr. GREEN CRÈME DE MENTHE

Shake Crème de Menthe and brandy, and strain into cocktail glass to serve.

BOSOM CARESSER

⅔ msr. BRANDY	1 teaspoon GRENADINE
⅓ msr. ORANGE CURAÇAO	CRACKED ICE
1 EGG YOLK	

Shake ice with brandy, curaçao, egg yolk and Grenadine. Strain into double cocktail glass and serve.

Left to right: Brandy Alexander, Coffee, Devil, Bosom Caresser.

Slaves working on British West Indies plantations during the 1600's created a new sugar cane by-product, and this was a raw spirit which they called Rumbullion (meaning 'rumpus'). Over the years Rumbullion has been refined and sophisticated into that which we call Rum.

It has warmed the hearts and souls of men exposed to the mercies of the elements, been the subject of sea-shanties, and served for several types of medicinal purposes.

Being composed mainly of sugar cane by-products, rum is produced in most of the world's sugar cane growing countries such as Venezuela, Brazil, Australia, Jamaica, Puerto Rico . . .

The leaves of the cane are stripped from the plant and crushed into juice. Water is removed from the juice to leave behind a syrup, which in turn is processed into a substance known as molasses. The molasses are further processed, the final extract being used for the distillation of rum. After distillation rum requires a maturation period of about three years.

Differing methods of distillation, type of caramel colouring agent used or the strain of yeast used in the processing can each contribute among other things to the variable qualities and characteristics of the types of rum which are available.

Traditional Jamaican Rum is dark and heavily bodied, very aromatic and possessing a strong flavour. Puerto Rican Rum on the other hand is an example of a light bodied rum.

SEE THROUGH

1 msr. BARCARDI WHITE RUM	1 dash BOLS BLUE CURAÇAO
½ msr. COINTREAU	1 COCKTAIL ONION
½ msr. ORANGE GIN	CRACKED ICE

Gently stir Bacardi, Cointreau, curaçao and gin into mixing glass which is half-filled with cracked ice. Strain off into cocktail glass and garnish with onion to serve.

DAIQUIRI

3 msrs. WHITE BACARDI	3 dashes GOMME SYRUP
1 msr. LEMON or LIME JUICE	or . . . 1 teaspoon SUGAR

Shake together Bacardi, the lemon (or lime) juice and Gomme syrup (or sugar, if preferred). To serve, strain off into a chilled cocktail glass.

RUM PERFECT

3 msrs. WHITE (or GOLDEN) RUM	1 slice LEMON PEEL
½ msr. dry FRENCH VERMOUTH	ICE CUBES
½ msr. sweet ITALIAN VERMOUTH	

Pour rum and both vermouths over ice in mixing glass. Stir briskly and pour off into a chilled martini glass. Drop in twist of lemon before serving.

RICO CHICO

2 msrs. DARK RUM	1 teaspoon SUGAR
1 msr. GIN	1 slice LEMON RIND
DRY GINGER ALE	CRACKED ICE

Having made sugar syrup, pour this with rum and gin over ice in shaker. Shake until frosty, and pour unstrained directly into a Collins glass. Top up with ginger ale. Garnish with fruit before serving.

Left to right: See-Through, Daiquiri, Rum Perfect, Rico Chico.

ZOMBIE (Simple)

1 msr. DARK RUM	1 msr. WHITE RUM
1 msr. JAMAICAN RUM	4 dashes CHERRY BRANDY
1 msr. LEMON or LIME JUICE	CRACKED ICE
4 dashes PASSION FRUIT and ORANGE JUICE	slice of ORANGE
4 dashes APRICOT BRANDY	GREEN and RED CHERRIES for decor

Top up zombie glass with cracked ice. Stir in all the ingredients and any decorative items. Decorate with cherries and the orange slice and serve with two drinking straws.

Left to right: Zombie (simple), Blue Hawaiian, Liberty, Ed's Baby.

BLUE HAWAIIAN

1 msr. WHITE RUM	1 msr. COCONUT CREAM
½ msr. BLUE CURAÇAO	CRUSHED ICE
2 msrs. PINEAPPLE JUICE	

One for the electric liquidizer, so make sure ice is well cracked or crushed. Add all ingredients to cracked ice in liquidizer and blend. Pour and serve in large-bowled glass.

LIBERTY

½ msr. WHITE RUM	1 dash GOMME SYRUP
1 msr. APPLEJACK BRANDY	CRACKED ICE

Stir ice in mixing glass with rum, Applejack brandy and Gomme syrup. Stir until cold and strain off into cocktail glass to serve.

ED'S BABY

½ msr. RUM	2 dashes BANANA LIQUEUR
¼ msr. CHERRY BRANDY	juice of 1 LIME
¼ msr. CURAÇAO	CRACKED ICE

Shake ice with rum, cherry brandy, curaçao, banana liqueur and lime juice. Strain off into glass and serve.

MONTEGO BAY

3 msrs. WHITE (or GOLDEN) RUM	1 sprig fresh MINT
1 msr. CRÈME DE MENTHE	CRACKED ICE
juice of ½ LEMON or LIME	

Add rum, Crème de Menthe and fruit juice to ice in shaker and shake until frosty. Strain off into a sour glass, and garnish with mint to serve.

PINA FRIA

2 msrs. WHITE RUM	3 dashes ANGOSTURA BITTERS
1 msr. PINEAPPLE JUICE	CRACKED ICE

Pour rum, pineapple juice, and bitters over ice in shaker. Shake until very frosty, and strain off to serve in sour glass.

FROZEN DAIQUIRI

It was so cold that the water bed had frozen solid.
She sat on the edge. It brought colour to her cheeks.
"I never thought it would be like this," she said icily.
I gave her a cold smile and a rum cocktail to match.
"This will make you melt," I said.
"I doubt it." She shook her frozen curls.
But later, things did get better. Just as I knew they would.
After all, no matter how cold the refrigerator, the light always comes on when you open the door.

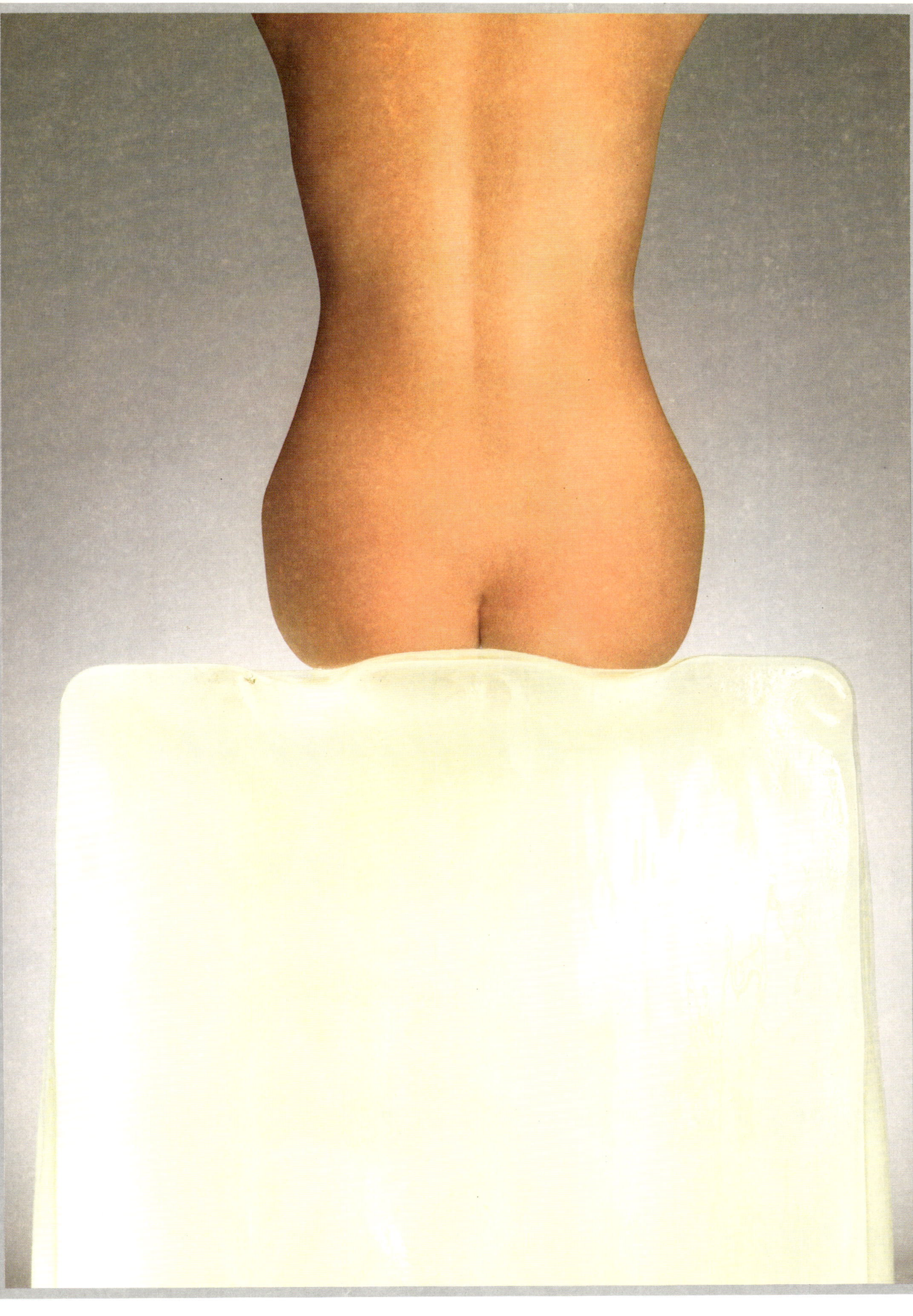

ZOMBIE (original)

2 msrs. LIGHT RUM	1 teaspoon PAPYA NECTAR
1 msr. JAMAICAN RUM	1 teaspoon PINEAPPLE JUICE
½ msr. APRICOT BRANDY	1 teaspoon PASSION FRUIT JUICE
½ teaspoon POWDERED SUGAR	1 teaspoon PLUM or APRICOT JUICE
½ msr. LEMON JUICE	CRACKED ICE
	MINT, PINEAPPLE and CHERRY (for decoration)

With the exception of any decorative items, place all the ingredients with ice into a shaker and mix well together. Half-fill a zombie glass with cracked ice and pour in the unstrained mix after shaking. Decorate with mint sprig, pineapple spear and cherry. Pop in two drinking straws and serve.

PLANTER'S PUNCH

2 msrs. JAMAICAN RUM	SODA WATER
1 msr. LEMON or LEMON JUICE	ICE
1 dash ANGOSTURA BITTERS	1 MARASCHINO CHERRY
1 teaspoon GRENADINE	LEMON or ORANGE slices

Pour rum, bitters, Grenadine and lemon (or lime) juice into glass containing ice and top up with soda water. Serve with two straws, after garnishing with cherry and slice of lemon (or orange, as perferred).

MAI TAI

2 msrs. LIGHT RUM	sprig of MINT
1 msr. JAMAICAN RUM	CRUSHED ICE
½ msr. ALMOND LIQUEUR	PINEAPPLE SPEAR
½ msr. LEMON or LIME JUICE	1 MARASCHINO CHERRY

Half-fill double old-fashioned glass with ice and mix in both rums, sugar, almond liqueur and lemon juice (or lime, if preferred). Fill up glass with crushed ice and stir all contents gently. Finish off by garnishing with sprig of mint, pineapple spear and cherry.

Left to right: Zombie (original), Pina Colada, Planter's Punch, Mai Tai.

PINA COLADA

1½ msrs. WHITE RUM	1 msr. COCONUT MILK
1 msr. PINEAPPLE JUICE	½ msr. CREAM
ICE	1 MARASCHINO CHERRY
	PINEAPPLE SLICE

Shake ice with rum, pineapple juice, coconut milk and cream. Strain off into champagne glass. To serve, garnish with a cherry and slice of pineapple.

BACARDI COCKTAIL

3 msrs. WHITE BACARDI	1 dash GRENADINE
1 msr. LEMON JUICE	1 MARASCHINO CHERRY
1 dash EGG WHITE	

Shake together Bacardi, lemon juice, egg white and Grenadine. Strain off into cocktail glass, garnish with cherry on a toothpick and serve.

BANANA COW

1½ msrs. CREAM	dash of GRENADINE
1 msr. CRÈME DE BANANE	NUTMEG
1 msr. WHITE RUM	ICE

Shake ice with cream, rum, Grenadine and Crème de Banana. Strain into cocktail glass, sprinkle nutmeg on top and serve.

HOT BUTTERED RUM

1½ msrs. JAMAICAN RUM	small slice BUTTER
1 lump SUGAR	NUTMEG
BOILING WATER	

Place silver spoon in old-fashioned glass to prevent breakage when topping up with boiling water, after mixing in rum, sugar and butter. Sprinkle nutmeg on top before serving.

Left to right: Bacardi, Banana Cow, Hot Buttered Rum, Frozen Daiquiri.

FROZEN DAIQUIRI

Same recipe as for Daiquiri (see Page 84) but serve with two straws in champagne glass of shaved ice.

ROARING RIVER

2 msrs. RUM	SODA WATER
1 msr. GIN	1 teaspoon SUGAR
3 dashes ANGOSTURA BITTERS	CRACKED ICE
½ teaspoon GRENADINE	

Splash bitters over ice in shaker and pour in rum, gin, Grenadine, and sugar water. Shake until frosty, and then pour unstrained directly into a Collins glass. Top up with soda water to serve.

PORT ANTONIO

3 msrs. WHITE (or GOLDEN) RUM	1 slice LIME PEEL
1 msr. LIME JUICE	ICE CUBES
½ teaspoon GRENADINE	

Pour rum, lime juice, and Grenadine over ice in mixing glass. Stir, and strain off into chilled martini glass, adding lime twist before serving.

SEE THRU

It's Friday evening. It's been a long, hard week.

You've just got home, mixed yourself a drink and put your feet up.

You settle down to the crossword.

Then, from across the street comes a tantalising glimpse through a lighted window.

It lasts for only a second. Yet in that moment you admire every delicious curve, every secret nook and cranny.

Then it's over. With a wry smile and a sip of your drink, it's back to the crossword.

One across, to look without buying (6, 8):
Window Shopping.

MOOMBA COCKTAIL

¾ msr. BACARDI RUM	¼ msr. LEMON JUICE
¾ msr. GRAND MARNIER	1 dash GRENADINE
½ msr. ORANGE JUICE	slice of ORANGE PEEL
CRACKED ICE	

Shake ice with rum, Grand Marnier and both juices with a dash of Grenadine and strain off into cocktail glass. Add orange peel and serve.

NIGHT LIGHT

⅔ msr. WHITE RUM	1 EGG YOLK
⅓ msr. ORANGE CURAÇAO	CRACKED ICE

Shake ice with rest of ingredients, strain off and pour into large cocktail glass to serve.

Left to right: Moomba, Night Light, Petite Fleur, Red Sunset.

PETITE FLEUR

⅓ msr. WHITE RUM	⅓ msr. GRAPEFRUIT JUICE
⅓ msr. COINTREAU	CRACKED ICE

Shake ice with remaining ingredients, strain off and serve.

RED SUNSET

½ msr. WHITE RUM	¼ msr. LEMON JUICE
½ msr. MANSIKKA LIQUEUR	CRACKED ICE

Shake ice with rum, liqueur and lemon juice. Strain off into cocktail glass and serve.

SCARLET LADY

¼ msr. BACARDI WHITE RUM	¼ msr. LEMON JUICE
¼ msr. CAMPARI	2 teaspoons MARASCHINO
¼ msr. MANDARINE LIQUEUR	ORANGE PEEL
CRACKED ICE	

Shake ice with rum, Campari, liqueur, lemon juice, Maraschino and strain off into cocktail glass. Add orange peel to rim of glass for decoration before serving.

SMILING THROUGH

⅓ msr. RUM	1 dash LEMON JUICE
⅓ msr. GRAND MARNIER	1 dash GRENADINE
⅓ msr. MARASCHINO	1 MARASCHINO CHERRY
CRACKED ICE	

Shake ice with rum, Grand Marnier, Maraschino, adding also dashes of lemon juice and Grenadine. Strain into cocktail glass and add cherry to serve.

Left to right: Scarlet Lady, Smiling Through, White Lily, Sweet Blondy.

WHITE LILY

⅓ msr. WHITE RUM	1 dash PASTIS
⅓ msr. COINTREAU	ICE
⅓ msr. GIN	

Put ice in mixing glass and add all ingredients. Stir until quite cold and strain into cocktail glass to serve.

SWEET BLONDY

⅓ mrs. LIGHT RUM	1 dash ORANGE JUICE
⅓ msr. MINT CHOCOLATE LIQUEUR	twist of ORANGE PEEL
⅓ msr. BIANCO VERMOUTH	CRACKED ICE

Shake ice with rum, liqueur, vermouth and orange juice. Strain off into cocktail glass and add twist of orange peel before serving.

CHAMPAGNE

Champagne takes its name from the small region of France just north of Paris, and apart from any associations which this exciting drink has with glamour and romance, it is without doubt one of the finest of wines. The chalky foundations upon which the Champagne countryside stands provide an ideal base for the cultivation of vines, and a mixture of two of the five varieties authorised for the region provide the grapes from which most champagnes are made. With a sugary and colourless juice the purple black pinot noir variety is said to give the wine plenty of body and a long life. The smaller golden chardonnay grape provides the wine with subtlety and a perfume.

The legal minimum ageing period for non-vintage champagne is one year, but the best are those which have been left to mature for between three to five years.

The three main areas of champagne production are Montagne de Reims, Vallée de la Marne and Côte des Blancs. Between them, many types of fine champagnes are produced. All are delicate, and whatever the type, they require correct and careful storage if they are to be preserved in prime condition. Even then, champagne loses its flavour if served too cold; serve too warm and it loses sparkle and becomes heavy. Before serving it should always be chilled, but never iced.

VERMOUTH

Vermouths are basically wines and therefore will soon deteriorate once the bottles have been opened. Sweet vermouths may last out for a month at the most after opening, and the dry varieties will be lucky to survive for half that time.

Although vermouth derives its name from that of the herb *Wermuth*, which is German for 'wormwood', it is from the French and the Italians that we have come to expect the finest vermouths. The French vermouth industry centres around Marseilles, and though generally associated with the lighter, drier varieties they produce either sweet or dry, and both have a spicey aroma. Primarily associated with the sweeter, heavier vermouths, the Italians also produce both types. Additionally, almost every wine-producing country in the world also produces vermouth, but mainly it is only for local consumption.

DUBONNET COCKTAIL

½ msr. DUBONNET	twist of LEMON
½ msr. GIN	ICE

Stir ice with Dubonnet and gin. Strain off into cocktail glass and garnish with lemon twist to serve.

Left to right: Dubonnet, Maria, French Greenery, Black Power.

MARIA

2 msrs. SWEET SHERRY	1 MARASCHINO CHERRY
1 msr. BEEFEATER'S GIN	3 cubes ICE

Place ice cubes in mixing glass, and stir in sherry and gin. Strain off into cocktail glass adding cherry for decoration before serving.

FRENCH GREENERY

1 msr. PERNOD	sprig of MINT
1 msr. GREEN CRÈME DE MENTHE	3 cubes ICE

Pour Crème de Menthe and Pernod over ice cubes placed in old-fashioned glass and add mint for decor before serving.

BLACK POWER

2 msrs. MARSALA WINE	COCA-COLA
slice of LEMON	3 cubes ICE

Pour Marsala over ice cubes placed in old-fashioned glass. Top up with Coca-Cola and add slice of lemon before serving.

CHAMPAGNE COBBLER

chilled CHAMPAGNE	½ teaspoon LEMON JUICE
1 slice of ORANGE	½ teaspoon CURAÇAO
CRACKED ICE	

Half-fill large glass with cracked ice, adding curaçao and lemon juice. Stir, adding orange slice and topping up until approximately two-thirds full with chilled champagne.

CHAMPAGNE COCKTAIL

chilled CHAMPAGNE	1 cube SUGAR
½ msr. BRANDY	twist of LEMON
ANGOSTURA BITTERS	

Place sugar cube in champagne glass and thoroughly soak with bitters. Add brandy and top up with chilled champagne. Stir gently to dissolve sugar lump, and add lemon twist before serving.

Left to right: Champagne Cobbler, Champagne, Fraise Royale, Champagne Napoleon.

FRAISE ROYALE

chilled CHAMPAGNE	2 fresh STRAWBERRIES
1 dash FRAISE LIQUEUR	

Strawberries are first blended with Fraise liqueur and then poured into a champagne glass. Top up glass with chilled champagne and serve.

CHAMPAGNE NAPOLEON

chilled CHAMPAGNE	1 dash ORANGE JUICE
1 msr. MANDARINE NAPOLEON	

Pour Mandarine Napoleon into champagne glass and add a dash of orange juice. To serve, top up glass with chilled champagne.

CAP FERRAT

3 msrs. DRY RED WINE	juice of 1 LEMON
1 dash PERNOD	ICE CUBES
1 teaspoon SUGAR SYRUP	

Pour wine, lemon juice and sugar syrup over ice in mixing glass. Stir well and strain off into a glass. Add dash of Pernod before serving.

RED LADY

3 msrs. RED WINE	ICE CUBES
1 msr. VODKA	

Stir wine and vodka together with ice in mixing glass and strain off to serve in a chilled martini glass.

AMERICANO

She promised to explain grid iron football, step by step.

First she took me to a ritzy cocktail bar just outside Dallas. I think it was called Southfork or something.

She suggested I tried an Americano.

I returned her steady gaze and said I was completely in favour. Anyway, it turned out to be some kind of Champagne cocktail.

Later, in the gym, padded from head to toe, she drawled: "When you hear the whistle, knock me down as quickly as you can."

I was only too happy to oblige. But I'll admit I was confused.

You see, I'd always thought that to bowl a maiden over was part of another quite different kind of game.

Rawlings
U.S.A.
CP36
CRUSADER

HAPPY YOUTH

chilled CHAMPAGNE	1½ msrs. ORANGE JUICE
½ msr. CHERRY BRANDY	1 lump SUGAR

Pour brandy over sugar lump placed in champagne glass and add orange juice. Top up with chilled champagne to serve.

FRENCH 75

chilled CHAMPAGNE	2 dashes GOMME SYRUP
¾ msr. GIN	ICE
¾ msr. fresh LEMON JUICE	

Shake gin and lemon juice and strain into tall, ice-filled glass. Top up with chilled champagne and serve.

Left to right: Happy Youth, French 75, Kir Royale, Mimosa.

KIR ROYALE

4 msrs. chilled CHAMPAGNE	2 dashes CRÈME DE CASSIS

Simply place 2 dashes of Crème de Cassis in champagne glass and top up with chilled champagne.

MIMOSA

chilled CHAMPAGNE	chilled ORANGE JUICE
1 dash ORANGE CURAÇAO	

Pour champagne and orange juice in equal parts into champagne glass and it's ready to serve (unless you'd fancy stirring in a dash of orange curaçao).

ALFONSO

chilled CHAMPAGNE	2 dashes ANGOSTURA BITTERS
1 msr. DUBONNET	twist of LEMON
1 lump SUGAR	

Shake bitters onto sugar lump placed in champagne glass. Add Dubonnet and top up with iced champagne. Stir gently, adding twist of lemon before serving.

BELLINI

chilled CHAMPAGNE	PEACH JUICE

Pour peach juice to fill one-third of champagne glass and top up with chilled champagne to serve.

Left to right: Alfonso, Bellini, Black Velvet, Buck's Fizz.

BLACK VELVET

chilled CHAMPAGNE	chilled STOUT

Pour both ingredients slowly, and in equal measures, into champagne or beer glass (or whatever size of drink you wish to serve).

BUCK'S FIZZ

chilled CHAMPAGNE	ORANGE JUICE
1 dash GRENADINE	

Pour fresh orange juice to fill one-third of champagne glass. Add dash of Grenadine (if desired) and top up with chilled champagne.

RITZ FIZZ

chilled CHAMPAGNE	1 dash clear LEMON JUICE
1 dash AMARETTO	1 ROSE PETAL for decor
1 dash BLUE CURAÇAO	

Mix amaretto, lemon juice and curaçao into champagne glass. Top up with champagne and decorate with rose petal to serve.

VALENCIA SMILE

chilled CHAMPAGNE	⅓ msr. ORANGE JUICE
⅔ msr. APRICOT BRANDY	4 dashes ORANGE BITTERS

Shake brandy, orange juice and bitters, and strain into champagne glass. To serve, top up with chilled champagne.

WALSH'S CHAMPAGNE COCKTAIL

chilled CHAMPAGNE	sprig fresh MINT
1 cube SUGAR	1 MARASCHINO CHERRY
twist of LEMON PEEL	CRUSHED ICE

Place sugar lump on top of ice-filled highball glass. Top up with champagne, decorating with mint, lemon peel and cherry to serve.

Left to right: Ritz Fizz, Valencia Smile, Walsh's Champagne.

AMERICANO COCKTAIL

2 msrs. SWEET VERMOUTH	3 cubes ICE
1 msr. CAMPARI BITTERS	twist of LEMON PEEL
SODA WATER	

Put ice cubes, vermouth and bitters into tall glass and top up with soda water. Add twist of lemon peel and stir before serving.

PINK PUSSY

½ msr. PEACH BRANDY	BITTER LEMON
1 msr. CAMPARI	CRACKED ICE
1 dash EGG WHITE	

Shake ice with peach brandy, egg white and Campari. Strain off into highball glass and top up with bitter lemon to serve.

PARIS MIST

3 msrs. DRY WHITE WINE	ICE CUBES
5 dashes of PERNOD	

Pour Pernod over ice in medium-sized glass, adding the wine and stirring gently before serving.

TIGER'S TAIL

2 msrs. PERNOD	8 msrs. chilled ORANGE JUICE

Place Pernod in tall highball glass, add orange juice and stir well before serving.

Left to right: Americano, Pink Pussy, Paris Mist, Tiger's Tail.

PARIS BY NIGHT

1 msr. PERNOD	1 MARASCHINO CHERRY
1 msr. STREGA	LEMONADE
½ msr. AMSTERDAM	1 slice of ORANGE

Place Pernod, Amsterdam and Strega in tall glass and top up with lemonade. Garnish with cherry and orange slice before serving.

PORT COCKTAIL

3 msrs. PORT	2 dashes ANGOSTURA BITTERS
1 teaspoon CURAÇAO	ICE CUBES

Pour port, Angostura bitters and curaçao over ice in mixing glass and stir briskly. Strain off to serve in a chilled martini glass.

SENSATION

3 msrs. PORT	1 slice LEMON PEEL
1 msr. BRANDY	ICE CUBES

Stir port and brandy briskly with ice in mixing glass. Strain off into a chilled martini glass, and garnish with lemon peel before serving.

PARIS BY NIGHT

There are two ways to improve your French vocabulary.

You can settle down at home with a dictionary and do it methodically.

Or you can do it with a little more style, and visit Paris. Preferably by night.

With any luck, whilst sipping cocktails by the Seine, you might meet up with a new friend.

In which case you can build an Arc de Triomphe of your own.

All the time, of course, your French vocabulary will be improving apace.

By the time you come home, those tricky French words such as camiknickers simply won't hold quite so much mystery.

CIGARETTES
BASTOS

Apart from Champagne Cocktails, there are names for other recognised categories into which mixed drinks are grouped, and it is a wise home mixologist and entertainer who becomes familiar with their names, and what they mean. They're all part of the bartender's language.

SLINGS

Whilst the original Slings of days gone by used gin, some recipes developed more recently recommend the alternative use of whisky or brandy as base ingredients. Usually served in a tall highball glass, Slings are created to provide a long, quenching drink.

As the early Gin Slings were considered by some to have evolved from Singapore, you might begin by experimenting with the following recipe. . .

SINGAPORE SLING

2 msrs. GIN	sprig of MINT
1 msr. CHERRY BRANDY	SODA WATER
1 msr. LEMON JUICE	slice of LEMON or ORANGE

Place gin, Cherry Brandy and lemon juice in tall highball glass and top up with soda water. Before serving garnish with fruit slice and sprig of mint.

SMASHES

Similar to a Collins drink, a Smash resembles a small type of Julep, containing spirit with mint and sugar. Smashes are served in an old-fashioned glass.

BRANDY SMASH

2 msrs. BRANDY	2 sprigs MINT
1 teaspoon SUGAR	CRACKED ICE
WATER	

Place a little water in old-fashioned glass to dissolve sugar. Muddle with mint sprigs, adding cracked ice. Pour in brandy, decorate with mint and serve with straws.

FRAPPÉS

Frappés are made from any liquor or liqueur or combination of same, though they are generally preferred with only one ingredient. They are always simply served with finely crushed ice.

Any Frappé can be prepared by simply filling a large cocktail glass with crushed ice and pouring in whatever measure you desire of any liquor or liqueur. Frappés are generally served with short straws.

SOURS

Almost any alcoholic ingredient may be used as a base for Sours, which depend for their sharp individuality upon the use of fresh fruit juices. They are generally served in 6oz. glasses.

WHISKY SOUR

2 msrs. SCOTCH WHISKY	1 MARASCHINO CHERRY
1 msr. LEMON JUICE	few drops EGG WHITE
½ teaspoon SUGAR	slice of ORANGE
SODA WATER	

Shake together whisky, lemon juice, sugar and egg white. Strain off into double-size cocktail glass or any 6oz. glass and fill with soda water. Top with cherry and orange slice before serving.

TODDIES

A toddy is still reserved by some for 'medicinal purposes only', though few will argue that it's a refreshing drink for the healthy and the hearty. Whether served hot or cold, Toddy recipes usually prescribe whisky, or any preferred spirit with a flavouring of lemon and the addition of other individual ingredients.

HOT TODDY

1½ msrs. ANY SPIRIT	1 slice LEMON
1 teaspoon SUGAR	1 stick CINNAMON
2 CLOVES	BOILING WATER

Mix spirit together with sugar, cloves, lemon slice and cinnamon in old-fashioned glass or mug. Place silver spoon in glass or mug (to prevent cracking) and pour in boiling water. It's now ready to serve.

Left to right: Singapore Sling, Brandy Smash, Whisky Sour, Hot Toddy.

COBBLERS

Cobblers are drinks usually made by pouring the ingredients into an ice-filled glass and topping off the presentation with a decorative sprig of mint, or fruit, before serving with straws.

SPIRIT COBBLERS

any chosen SPIRIT	1 teaspoon SUGAR
4 dashes ORANGE CURAÇAO	CRACKED ICE
any FRUIT IN SEASON	sprig of MINT

Add rum, gin, whisky, gin or brandy (as preferred) to medium or large wine glass which has been filled with ice. Amount varies according to strength required. Stir the sugar and curaçao well before decorating with fruit, topping with a sprig of mint, and serving with two straws.

COLLINS

These are long, refreshing drinks, served in a tall highball glass, with plenty of ice. Gin-based, there are countless recipes for this type of mixed drink which is believed by some to have originated in Britain.

Some recommend substituting rum, brandy, or whisky for the gin ingredient. Others claim a Collins recipe need not always be stirred, but can, after the addition of egg white, be shaken and then topped with soda before serving.

The name is believed to have been derived from John Collins, a 19th century London waiter famous for serving his customers a particular type of mixed drink. At one time, a 'John Collins' was mixed using Dutch gin, and a 'Tom Collins' called for the use of 'Old Tom' gin. Nowadays, both drinks can be acceptably made with London Dry gin.

JOHN (or TOM) COLLINS

2 msrs. DRY GIN	SODA WATER
2 msrs. LEMON JUICE	slice of LEMON
CRACKED ICE	1 MARASCHINO CHERRY
1 teaspoon SUGAR	1 teaspoon GOMME SYRUP

Place ample ice in highball glass. Add gin, lemon juice and syrup. Top up with soda water and stir well. Serve with slice of lemon and straws.

CRUSTAS

Crustas are usually served in a champagne glass, or goblet, the rim of which has been moistened with a slice of lemon before being dipped in sugar to give a frosted appearance. Brandy is the most popular ingredient used in making these kind of drinks.

BRANDY CRUSTA

3 msrs. BRANDY	3 dashes MARASCHINO
1 dash ANGOSTURA BITTERS	1 MARASCHINO CHERRY

Shake brandy with bitters and Maraschino. Strain off into champagne glass, add cherry on top and serve.

(This recipe can also be tried with the addition of 1 teaspoon lemon juice and 2 teaspoons orange juice.)

COOLERS

Coolers are very similar to Collins, being long refreshing drinks which are ideal for serving on hot summer days. A Cooler, though, usually contains the spiralled peel of any fruit ingredient.

RUM COOLER

2 msrs. RUM	SODA WATER
2 msrs. LEMON JUICE	CRACKED ICE
4 dashes GRENADINE	FRUIT

Shake ice with rum, Grenadine and lemon juice. Strain off into glass, add cracked ice and top up with soda water. Garnish with citrus fruit and a spiral of peel to serve.

HIGHBALLS

American folklore tells us that when workmen were building their railroads they knew it was time to down tools for a rest and a refreshing drink as soon as they saw a white disc being raised high upon a pole to signify the stoppage. Since then, Highball has become a name for any long, thirst-quenching drink.

HORSE'S NECK

1½ msrs. BRANDY	DRY GINGER ALE
2 dashes ANGOSTURA BITTERS	4 cubes of ICE
1 whole LEMON	

Remove the skin of the lemon carefully in one piece and place one end of the broad strip as firmly as possible over the edge of a tall highball glass so that the rest of it hangs over to give the effect of a horse's neck. Add ice cubes to glass, followed by brandy and bitters before topping up with dry ginger ale and serving.

Left to right: Brandy Cobbler, John Collins, Brandy Crusta, Rum Cooler.

FLIPS

Once popular with seamen, who particularly fancied the rum-based Flips, these drinks are close to Egg Nogs. They differ mainly in the fact that Flip recipes do not contain milk as an ingredient.

BRANDY FLIP

2 msrs. BRANDY	CRACKED ICE
1 teaspoon SUGAR	NUTMEG
1 EGG	

Shake ice with brandy, sugar and egg. Strain off into medium-size wine glass and sprinkle nutmeg on top before serving.

(This basic Flip recipe can be used to provide a number of different drinks, substituting gin, whisky, rum, brandy, port, sherry or claret for the brandy ingredient).

GIMLET

In the days of the old sailing ships, sailors were encouraged to eat fresh limes to increase their intake of Vitamin C, and thereby becoming protected from scurvy. Consumption became the more palatable if the juice of the lime was mixed with a tot of gin, and that's how the Gimlet came about (or, that's how the story goes, anyway!).

JULEPS

This range of mixed drinks is accredited to the planters of the southern states of the USA where many varieties were evolved early in the 19th century. They remain generally popular mainly because of their refreshing mint ingredient.

OLD GEORGIA JULEP

1 msr. PEACH or APRICOT BRANDY	CRACKED ICE
1 lump SUGAR	4 leaves of MINT

Dissolve sugar in a little water in tall highball glass. Add mint leaves and muddle together before adding brandy. Fill glass with cracked ice and stir gently before serving.

Left to right: Old Georgia Julep, Gimlet, Brandy Flip, Horse's Neck.

FIZZES

More relatives of the Collins family of drinks, but these are always shaken and should be consumed as soon as possible after preparation to avoid loss of flavour.

BACARDI FIZZ

2 msrs. BACARDI RUM	CRACKED ICE
2 msrs. LEMON JUICE	SODA WATER
1 teaspoon SUGAR	

Shake ice with rum, lemon juice and sugar. Strain off into highball glass and top up with soda water to serve.

DAISIES

Whilst Daisies can contain any sort of spirit, they require vigorous shaking to ensure maximum coldness, preserving the chill still further by serving in glasses, or goblets, full of cracked ice. Recipes usually recommend lavish decoration with fruit, to complete a quenching summer drink.

BRANDY DAISY

2 msrs. BRANDY	6 dashes GRENADINE
1 msr. LEMON JUICE	SODA WATER
CRACKED ICE	MINT and FRUIT decor

Shake brandy, Grenadine and lemon juice and strain off into goblet full of cracked ice. Add soda water and decorate with sprigs of mint and slices of fruit in season.

BLACK POWER

We met at the Club.

It was obvious from the way she danced that she was very fit.

We talked about everything from power-lifting to aerobics. And when she described her evening routine of callisthenics, I broke out in a cold sweat.

With a wry smile, she introduced me to the delights of a cocktail called Black Power. It was as smooth and supple as she was.

Finally, at about two, she suggested softly that we should go back to her place. I agreed gladly.

What I didn't realise, of course, was that her place was a gymnasium.

Frankly, though, I can't remember having had so much fun keeping fit.

TEQUILA STRAIGHT

1½ msrs. TEQUILA	1 slice LEMON
SALT	

Hold shot glass in your right hand. Hold lemon slice between finger and thumb of left hand, with small deposit of salt already placed on side of hand, near thumb. Lick up the salt, drink the Tequila, and finally bite into the lemon.

MARGARITA

1½ msrs. TEQUILA	slice of LEMON
1 msr. Fresh LEMON or LIME JUICE	SALT
½ msr. TRIPLE SEC or COINTREAU	

First prepare glass by moistening rim with lemon slice and then sprinkling salt over moistened area to give crusted effect on rim. Shake Tequila with Triple Sec (or Cointreau) and lemon (or lime) juice. Strain off into prepared cocktail glass and garnish with slice of lemon before serving.

(Some claim that this cocktail was named after a beautiful Mexican dancer, famous for her flashing eyes and tapping feet.)

TEQUILA COCKTAIL

2 msrs. TEQUILA	1 dash EGG WHITE
4 dashes GRENADINE	ICE
juice of ½ LEMON	twist of LEMON

Shake ice with Tequila, lemon juice, Grenadine and egg white. Strain off into cocktail glass and garnish with twist of lemon before serving.

Left to right: Tequila Straight, Margarita, Tequila.

EGG NOGG

10 msrs. MILK	ICE
1 EGG	NUTMEG or CINNAMON
1 teaspoon CASTOR SUGAR	1 MARASCHINO CHERRY

Shake ice with egg, castor sugar and milk. Strain into tall highball glass. Dust with nutmeg or cinnamon, garnish with cherry and serve with drinking straw.

MICKEY MOUSE

1 scoop ICE CREAM	WHIPPED CREAM
ICE	2 MARASCHINO CHERRIES
COCA-COLA	

Pour Coca-Cola into tall glass containing some ice and add scoop of ice cream. Top up with whipped cream, adding two cherries and a straw and providing spoon when serving.

LEMONADE

juice of 1 LEMON	1 slice of LEMON
CRACKED ICE	WATER
2 tablespoons SUGAR	

Add lemon juice and sugar to tall glass filled with cracked ice. Shake, and pour unstrained into glass. Top up with water, add slice of lemon and serve with straws.

Left to right: Egg Nogg, Mickey Mouse, Lemonade, Boo Boo's Special.

BOO BOO'S SPECIAL

3 msrs. PINEAPPLE JUICE	ICE
3 msrs. ORANGE JUICE	1 dash ANGOSTURA BITTERS
¼ msr. LEMON JUICE	1 dash GRENADINE
WATER	PINEAPPLE or seasonal FRUIT

Shake ice with Angostura bitters, Grenadine, lemon, pineapple and orange juices. Serve in tall, highball glass and top up with water. Before serving, garnish with pineapple, or any fruit in season.

ANITA

3 msrs. ORANGE JUICE	SODA WATER
1 msr. LEMON JUICE	seasonal FRUIT
2 dashes ANGOSTURA BITTERS	CRACKED ICE

Shake ice with fruit juices and bitters and strain off into highball glass. Top up with soda water, add fruit decor, and serve with straws.

SAINT CLEMENTS

ORANGE JUICE	slice of ORANGE
BITTER LEMON	slice of LEMON
ICE CUBES	

Place ice cubes in large whisky glass. Top up with equal parts of orange and lemon juices. Stir vigorously and garnish with fruit slices to serve.

TIGER'S TAIL

A romantic weekend away in an ancient country seat.

With a huge open hearth, a roaring fire, and an inviting tiger skin rug.

You lock the doors and dim the lights. Now for that safari.

She flicks the tiger's tail. You take the hint and mix her a drink.

Side by side, you sit and sip.

Then, suddenly, there's a distant roar. The whole room sways.

An earthquake? No, you're near a safari park.

And inside that lovely smooth tiger skin . . . there's a tiger.

The bad news is, he's a mantotaller.

SHIRLEY TEMPLE

GINGER ALE	1 MARASCHINO CHERRY
1-2 dashes of GRENADINE	ICE CUBES

Pour ginger ale over ice cubes in tall highball glass and stir in one or two dashes of Grenadine, the amount varying according to personal preferences. Add cherry, and serve.

ROSY PIPPIN

wine glass of APPLE JUICE	GINGER ALE
1 dash of GRENADINE	slice of APPLE
1 dash of LEMON JUICE	

Add dashes of Grenadine and lemon juice to wine glass of apple juice and stir briskly. Pour off unstrained into larger whisky glass and top up with ginger ale. Decorate with slice of apple wedged onto rim of glass, and serve.

Left to right: Shirley Temple, Rosy Pippin, Grecian, Pussyfoot.

GRECIAN

4 msrs. PEACH JUICE	SODA WATER
2 msrs. ORANGE JUICE	seasonal FRUIT
1 msr. LEMON JUICE	CRUSHED ICE

Place scoop of cracked or crushed ice in blender, and add the three fruit juices. Blend together and pour unstrained into a red wine glass. Add a dash of soda water, and garnish with fruit to serve.

PUSSYFOOT

1 msr. ORANGE JUICE	yolk of 1 EGG
1 msr. LIME JUICE	SODA WATER
1 msr. LEMON JUICE	1 MARASCHINO CHERRY
1 dash of GRENADINE	CRACKED ICE

Shake ice with orange, lemon and lime juices, to which has been added an egg yolk and a dash of Grenadine. Strain off into a red wine glass, adding a cherry for decor, and serving with straws.

CINDERELLA

1 msr. PINEAPPLE JUICE	chunk of PINEAPPLE
1 msr. LEMON JUICE	1 MARASCHINO CHERRY
1 msr. ORANGE JUICE	CRACKED ICE and CUBES
1 dash GRENADINE	SODA WATER

Shake cracked ice with pineapple, lemon and orange juices. Strain off over ice cubes in highball glass and top up with soda water. Add dash of Grenadine and garnish with pineapple chunk and cherry on a stick. Serve with straws.

NURSERY FIZZ

ORANGE JUICE	slice of ORANGE
GINGER ALE	1 MARASCHINO CHERRY
ICE CUBES	

Place ice in red wine glass and top up with equal parts of orange juice and ginger ale. Add slice of orange and a cherry for decor, and serve with straws.

CAPUCINE

4 msrs. FRESH CREAM	CHOCOLATE BAR
1 msr. PEPPERMINT CORDIAL	CRACKED and CRUSHED ICE

Shake cracked ice with peppermint cordial and cream and strain off into a red wine glass. Add crushed ice, and sprinkle grated chocolate over top of drink before serving.

JERSEY LILY

1 dash ANGOSTURA BITTERS	1 MARASCHINO CHERRY
½ teaspoon SUGAR SYRUP	ICE CUBES
fizzy APPLE JUICE	

Add bitters and sugar syrup to ice in mixing glass and stir in with just less than a red wine glass full of fizzy apple juice. Strain off into red wine glass and garnish with cherry before serving.

Left to right: Cinderella, Nursery Fizz, Capucine, Jersey Lily.

GLOSSARY

Numbers listed after each liqueur or spirit indicate the page on which a recipe may be found using this ingredient.

ADVOKAAT: A thick, custard-like, Dutch liqueur made from egg yolk, sugar and brandy. (47)

ALMOND LIQUEUR: A liqueur flavoured with almonds and sweetened. (88)

AMARETTO: An almond and apricot based liqueur, first made in Saronno, near Lake Como, Italy, during the 16th Century. (62, 77, 102).

AMSTERDAM: A liqueur containing Cherry Brandy and Advokaat. (104)

ANGOSTURA BITTERS: An infusion of aromatics from the West Indies, used very sparingly for flavouring cocktails and mixed drinks.

APPLEJACK BRANDY: A brandy distilled from cider apples, originating from New England, U.S.A. (76, 85)

AURUM: A pale golden, half dry liqueur, flavoured with orange. (20)

BANANA LIQUEUR: A liqueur flavoured with bananas and sweetened. (85)

BENEDICTINE: A sweet, golden coloured, brandy based liqueur, flavoured with mixed herbs and originally made by Benedictine monks from Fécamp, Normandy, France. (28, 43, 60, 68, 80)

BITTERS: An infusion of aromatics, usually prepared by blending aromatic or fruit substances with wine or spirit.

CALVADOS: An apple brandy from Normandy, France. (69)

CAMPARI BITTERS: An Italian aperitif wine with strong, bitter taste and very red colour. (29, 93, 103)

CHARTREUSE: a liqueur produced from over 130 different herbs and spices, originally produced by monks at La Grand Chartreuse Monastery, Grenoble, France. It can either be yellow, which is light, or green, which is greater in spirit strength. (20)

COINTREAU: A sweet, colourless liqueur flavoured with oranges and produced in Anjou, France. (22, 25, 26, 29, 33, 40, 51, 56, 58, 73, 76, 84, 92, 93, 114)

CRÈME DE BANANE: A pungent, banana flavoured liqueur, which can be either white or straw coloured. (58, 89)

CRÈME DE CACAO: A very sweet, brandy based liqueur, made from Venezuelan cocoa beans. It has a cocoa-vanilla flavour and is chocolate brown in colour. (33, 54, 81)

CRÈME DE CASSIS: A brandy based liqueur, flavoured with blackcurrants, originally from Dijon, France. (100)

CRÈME DE MENTHE: A peppermint flavoured liqueur, based on grain spirit, which can be green, white or pink. (21, 29, 34, 43, 44, 48, 64, 72, 74, 76, 81, 86, 96)

CRÈME DE NOYEAU: A sweet, bitter almond flavoured liqueur, made from peach and cherry kernels, and which can be either pink or white. (69, 77)

CRÈME YVETTE: The best known of the crème de violettes, it has the flavour, perfume and colour of Parma violets, and originates from the U.S.A. (24)

CURAÇAO: A sweet liqueur, which can be blue, white or orange, and which is made with peel of oranges, originally from Curaçao in the West Indies. The name is now applied to all orange flavoured liqueurs. (32, 46, 48, 69, 70, 72, 77, 78, 80, 81, 84, 85, 92, 97, 100, 102, 104, 109).

DRAMBUIE: A Scotch whisky based liqueur, flavoured with herbs and heather honey. (39, 68)

DUBONNET: A red wine based French aperitif. (32, 48, 51, 59, 77, 96, 101).

EAU DE VIE: A colourless, fruit brandy made by distillation of a fruit. The most famous ones comes from Alsace, France.

FERNET BRANCA: Italian Bitters made from alcohol mixed with essences extracted from plants, roots, stems and bark. (32)

FORBIDDEN FRUIT: A flame coloured, American liqueur made from Shaddock, a type of grapefruit, with a bittersweet, citrus flavour. (20, 34, 64)

FRAISE LIQUEUR: A liqueur flavoured with strawberries. (97)

GALLIANO: A golden coloured liqueur, flavoured with liquorice and aniseed, produced in Milan, Italy. (47, 55)

GOMME SYRUP: Sugar syrup

GRAND MARNIER: A Cognac brandy based liqueur, golden brown in colour, and flavoured with oranges. (33, 92, 93)

GRENADINE: A red, non-alcoholic, French fruit syrup made from Pomegranates, and possessing a slight redcurrant flavour.

KAHLUA: a rich brown liqueur made from Mexican Coffee beans. (55)

KIRSCH: A colourless, unsweetened fruit spirit distilled from cherries, with a bitter almond flavour. (69)

LAKKA LIQUEUR: A bittersweet liqueur made from cloudberries from Finland. Also known as Suomuurain. (58)

LILLET: A French, aromatized wine, produced in a similar way to vermouth, and served as an aperitif. (58, 69)

MANDARINE NAPOLEON: A Cognac and eau de vie based liqueur, flavoured with tangerine peel, from Belgium. (97)

MANDARINE LIQUEUR: A tangerine flavoured liqueur. (93)

MANSIKKA LIQUEUR: A strawberry flavoured liqueur from Finland. (92)

MARASCHINO: A colourless liqueur from Italy made with sour maraschino cherries and their crushed kernels. (72, 93, 109)

MARSALA WINE: A dark, fortified wine from Sicily. (96)

MINT CHOCOLATE LIQUEUR: A liqueur based on milk chocolate and peppermint. (93)

ORANGE GIN: Gin flavoured with orange peel. (84)

ORGEAT SYRUP: A non-alcoholic syrup made from almonds. (77)

PASTIS: A clear, liquorice based liqueur from Marseilles, France, which turns white when mixed with water. (48, 78, 93)

PERNOD: A dry, clear liqueur flavoured with aniseed, coriander, fennel, hyssop and liquorice, and which turns cloudy when mixed with water. (26, 34, 50, 51, 63, 68, 72, 96, 98, 103, 104)

PORT: A full bodied wine, fortified with brandy during fermentation, and which comes from the Duoro Valley in the north of Portugal. (58, 81, 104)

PRUNELLE: A pale green brandy, flavoured with sloe berries. (69)

SHERRY: A wine fortified with brandy, which is added after fermentation. Originally from Spain, it now comes also from Australia, South Africa and Cyprus. (29, 96)

SLOE GIN: A deep red liqueur, produced by steeping sloe berries in gin. (28)

STREGA: A light, golden coloured liqueur from Italy, flavoured with over 70 herbs and spices. (104)

STOUT: Thick, creamy, dark beer, which is produced by roasting the barley until black to add colour and flavouring, and made with a high proportion of malt and hops. (101)

SWEDISH PUNCH: A blend of rum, syrup, lemon and spices. (43)

TEQUILA: A clear spirit distilled in Mexico from a species of agave plant, similar to cactus. (114)

TRIPLE SEC: A white curaçao, which is colourless, flavoured with orange peel, and sweetened. (80, 114)

INDEX

Abbey Cocktail, 20
Adam and Eve, 47
Alaska Cocktail, 20
Alexander Cocktail No. 2, 33
Alfonso, 101
Alfonso Cocktail, 33
Algonquin, 50
Amelia's Rip Cord, 56
American Beauty, 80
Americano Cocktail, 103
Amsterdam Cocktail, 33
Anita, 116
Apricot Cocktail, 33
B & B, 80
Bacardi Cocktail, 89
Bacardi Fizz, 112
Balmoral, 68
Banana Cow, 89
Banjo, 63
Bellini, 101
Bessie and Jessie, 47
Between the Sheets, 80
Bikini, 56
Black Power, 96
Black Russian, 55
Black Velvet, 101
Blériot, 20
Blinker Cocktail, 47
Bloody Mary, 55
Blue Blazer, 40
Blue Hawaiian, 85
Blue Moon Cocktail, 24
Bobby Burns, 43
Boilermaker, 43
Bombay Cocktail, 80
Boo Boo's Special, 115
Boomerang Cocktail, 43
Borden, 50
Bosom Caresser, 81
Bourbon Mint Julep, 46
Brandy Alexander, 81
Brandy Crusta, 109
Brandy Daisy, 112
Brandy Flip, 111
Brandy Smash, 107
Bronx Cocktail, 24
Buck's Fizz, 101
Bullshot, 62
Burnt Orange, 73
Cap Ferrat, 98
Capucine, 119
Carlton Cocktail, 40
Carnival, 69
Champagne Cobbler, 97
Champagne Cocktail, 97
Champagne Napoleon, 97
Cherry Blossom, 69
Chi Chi, 62
Cinderella, 119
Clover Club Cocktail, 24
Coffee Cocktail, 81
Coronation Cocktail, 24
Corpse Reviver, 69
Cupid's Bow, 20
Daiquiri, 84
Delmonico, 22
Depth Bomb, 73
Deshler Cocktail, 51
Devil Cocktail, 81
Dubonnet Cocktail, 96
Edinburgh, 44
Ed's Baby, 85
Edward VIII Cocktail, 51
Egg Nogg, 115
Egg Sour, 70
Esquire, 73
Fallen Angel Cocktail, 21
Fascinator, 72
Fioupe, 68
Fixer, 69
Fraise Royale, 97
Frappés, 107
French 75 (Gin-based), 21
French 75 (Champagne-based), 100
French 95, 51
French 125, 70
French Connection, 77
French Greenery, 96
Frozen Daiquiri, 89
Gibson Dry, 32
Gibson Sweet, 21
Gilroy Cocktail, 21
Gimlet, 111
Godmother, 62
Grecian, 118
Happy Youth, 100
Harrity, 44
Harvey Wallbanger, 55
Haven, 63
Head-Over-Heels, 56
Here's How, 60
Horse's Neck, 110
Hot Buttered Rum, 89
Hot Toddy, 108
Inspiration, 60
Irish on the Rocks, 51
Jack in the Box, 76
Jerry's Joy, 58
Jersey Lily, 119
John Collins, 109
Kir Royale, 100
Klondike, 74
La Dame Blanche, 64
Lemonade, 115
Leprechaun Dancer, 38
Leviathan Cocktail, 76
Liberty, 85
Luigi, 22
Maiden, 64

Maiden's Prayer, 26
Mai Tai, 88
Mamie Taylor, 38
Manhattan (dry), 38
Manhattan (sweet), 38
Maple Leaf, 50
Margarita, 114
Maria, 96
Martini (dry), 32
Martini (sweet), 32
Mary Stuart, 68
Melbourne, 72
Mickey Mouse, 115
Millionaire, 77
Mimosa, 100
Monkey's Gland, 26
Montego Bay, 86
Monty Rosa, 73
Moomba Cocktail, 92
Morning, 72
Morning Glory, 39
Moscow Mule, 55
Napoleon Cocktail, 32
Negroni, 29
New Orleans Fizz, 30
New York Cocktail, 39
New Yorker Cocktail, 25
Night Light, 92
Nursery Fizz, 119
Old-Fashioned, 47
Old Georgia Julep, 111
Olympic, 77
Opossum, 59
Orange Blossom Cocktail, 25
Paris, 68
Paris by Night, 104
Paris Mist, 103
Perfect Cocktail, 25
Perth, 63
Petite Fleur, 92
Pina Colada, 88
Pina Fria, 86
Pink Gin, 25
Pink Lady, 28
Pink Pussy, 103
Planter's Punch, 88
Port Antonio, 90
Port Cocktail, 104
Prince, The, 74
Prize Idiot, 58
Pussyfoot, 118
Queen's Cocktail, 28
Ramoz Fizz, 30
Red Hackle, 77
Red Lady, 98
Red Sunset, 92
Rico Chico, 84
Ritz Fizz, 102
Roaring River, 90
Rob Roy, 39
Rolls Royce, 28
Rosy Pippin, 118
Rum Cooler, 110
Rum Perfect, 84
Russian Cocktail, 54
Rusty Nail, 39
Saint Clements, 116
St Kitts, 72
Salty Dog, 54
San Francisco, 28
Scarlet Lady, 93
Scotch Mist, 42
Screwdriver, 54
Seafoam, 63
See Through, 84
Sensation, 104
Sherry Cocktail, 29
Shirley Temple, 118
Side Car, 76
Singapore Sling, 107
Smiling Through, 93
Spirit Cobblers, 109
Stinger, 76
Stone, 50
Surf Rider, 59
Swan, 34
Sweet Blondy, 93
Temptation, 48
Tennessee Manhattan (dry), 42
Tennessee Snifter, 42
Tennessee Sour, 42
Tequila Cocktail, 114
Tequila Straight, 114
Thunder, 78
Tiger's Tail, 103
Tinker, 78
Tom Collins, 109
Upstairs, 58
Valencia Smile, 102
Virgin, 34
Virgin Cocktail, 29
Vodka Martini, 54
Vodka Mist, 62
Vodka Silver Fizz, 59
Vodka Zaza, 59
Walsh's Champagne Cocktail, 102
Ward 8, 46
Ward Eight, 46
Whip, 78
Whisky Cobbler, 46
Whisky Royal, 48
Whisky Sour, 108
White Elephant, 34
White Lady, 29
White Lily, 93
Whiz Bang, 43
Zombie (original), 88
Zombie (simple), 85

ACKNOWLEDGEMENTS

Photographer's Assistant: Dean Freeman
Stylist: Camilla Trowbridge
Make-up by Mary-Lou and Stephanie Walker
Hair by Ayo at Schumi

Cocktails prepared by John Duthie

The publishers would like to thank the following for their assistance:
Bollinger Champagne
Tanqueray Gordon & Company Limited
White Horse Distillers Limited
Charles Jourdan
Chaumet Jewellers, 178 New Bond Street, London W1.
Riva Furs, 67-69 George Street, London W1.

Glasses and Cocktail Accessories from The Cocktail Shop, 30 Neal Street, London WC2, and 5 Avery Row, Mayfair, London W1.

Photographs on pages 10, 11, 14 and 17 from Colour Library International.

Typesetting by RP Typesetters Limited, London.

Colour Separation by Newsele Litho Limited, Amersham.